The Foreign Policy Centre

GU00745942

The Foreign Policy Centre is an independent think-tank launched by Prime Minister Tony Blair (Patron) and former Foreign Secretary Robin Cook (President) to examine the impact of globalisation on foreign and domestic policy. The Centre has developed a distinctive research agenda that explores the strategic solutions needed to tackle issues which cut across borders – focusing on the legitimacy as well as the effectiveness of policy.

The Foreign Policy Centre has produced a range of **Publications** by key thinkers on subjects relating to the role of non-state actors in policymaking, the future of Europe, international security and identity. These include: *The Post-Modern State and the World Order* by Robert Cooper, *Network Europe* and *Going Public* by Mark Leonard, *NGOs Rights and Responsibilities* by Michael Edwards, *After Multiculturalism* by Yasmin Alibhai-Brown, *Trading Identities* by Wally Olins and *Third Generation Corporate Citizenship* by Simon Zadek.

The Centre runs a rich and varied **Events Programme** at The Mezzanine in Elizabeth House – a forum where representatives from NGOs, think-tanks, companies and government can interact with speakers who include prime ministers, Nobel Prize laureates, global corporate leaders, activists, media executives and cultural entrepreneurs from around the world.

The Centre's quarterly magazine, **Global Thinking**, is a regular outlet for new thinking on foreign policy issues. Features include profiles, exclusive interviews with decision makers, and opinion pieces by the Centre's permanent staff and associated authors.

The Centre runs a unique **Internship Programme** – the UK's only route for new graduates into the foreign policy arena.

For more information on these activities please visit **www.fpc.org.uk**

About the editor

Mark Leonard is Director of The Foreign Policy Centre. He has written widely on European integration and legitimacy including his acclaimed pamphlet *Network Europe* (Foreign Policy Centre 1999) and *The Pro-European Reader* (with Dick Leonard, Palgrave 2002). His work on "Rebranding Britain" led to an international debate on branding countries and inspired the Foreign Secretary to launch Panel 2000, a taskforce to advise him on promoting Britain abroad. Mark has built on this with influential studies on "public diplomacy" including the report *Going Public: Diplomacy for the Information Society* (with Vidhya Alakeson, Foreign Policy Centre 2000). Mark writes and broadcasts extensively on British, European and international politics. He has acted as a consultant on identity for foreign governments and private companies. Mark previously worked as senior researcher at the think-tank *Demos* and as a trainee journalist at *The Economist*.

Also by The Foreign Policy Centre:

Over the course of the first half of 2002, the Centre will be publishing a series of collections focusing on the repercussions of 11 September.

- **Global Britons: reflections on identity following 11 September** – a collection of essays by a group of leading thinkers on the subject of identity, including Yasmin Alibhai-Brown, David Blunkett, Philip Dodd, Adrienne Katz, Francesca Klug, David Lammy, Ziauddin Sardar and Michael Wills.

- **Tackling the new face of terrorism: the value of impact reduction** – a collection of essays with experts on the subject of risk, including contributions by Dr Sally Leivesley, John Smith of Prudential, David Veness QPM of the Metropolitan Police Service, and the Civil Contingencies Secretariat of the Cabinet Office.

Re-Ordering the World

Edited by
Mark Leonard

The Foreign Policy Centre

First published in 2002 by
The Foreign Policy Centre
The Mezzanine
Elizabeth House
39 York Road
London
SE1 7NQ

Email info@fpc.org.uk
www.fpc.org.uk

ISBN 1-903558-10-7

Cover by David Carroll

Typesetting by John and Michael Breeze

Re-Ordering the World

The Contributors

Ehud Barak is former Prime Minister of Israel.

Ulrich Beck is Professor of Sociology at the University of Munich.

Tony Blair is Prime Minister of Great Britain.

Fernando Henrique Cardoso is President of the Federative Republic of Brazil.

Malcolm Chalmers is Professor of International Politics at the University of Bradford.

Robert Cooper is a senior serving British diplomat.

Fred Halliday is Professor of International Relations at the London School of Economics.

David Held is Graham Wallas Professor of Political Science at the London School of Economics.

Mary Kaldor is Principal Research Fellow and Programme Director at the Centre for the Study of Global Governance at the London School of Economics.

Kanan Makiya is Professor in Near Eastern and Judaic Studies at Brandeis University.

Joseph Nye is dean of the Kennedy School of Government at Harvard University.

Amartya Sen is Master of Trinity College, University of Cambridge.

Jack Straw is Foreign Secretary of Great Britain.

Fareed Zakaria is Editor of *Newsweek.*

The views expressed in The Foreign Policy Centre publications are the views of the authors. This collection is published to further the Centre's aim of promoting debate about foreign policy and Britain's place in the world.

Acknowledgements

First of all, I would like to thank my fellow contributors for making this collection possible. Special thanks need to go to David Held for his generous advice and ideas. I would like to thank the people who helped draw the pamphlet together, especially Peter Hyman at 10 Downing Street and Ed Owen and Michael Williams at the Foreign Office. Many thanks to Sunder Katwala for his contribution to the original planning of the project. Once again, I am extremely grateful to John and Michael Breeze for typesetting the text and for David Carroll for his original cover idea.

At The Foreign Policy Centre, I need to thank the team of interns which is so crucial when it comes to making things happen. Special thanks need to go to Jonathan White for pulling the project together from its conception and to Conrad Smewing for seeing the project through. Particular thanks also due to Rob Blackhurst and Phoebe Griffith for taking responsibility for ensuring the project's final completion.

Mark Leonard   March 2002

Foreword by Tony Blair

The events of 11 September brought home the reality of globalisation to us all. By challenging our fundamental security and the very values on which our societies are based, they have increased fear and uncertainty about the future and also given a new urgency in the search for solutions.

This is the context in which this collection's authors write. Mark Leonard has drawn together a group of authors well qualified to assess current problems and to identify possible solutions. Together, these add up to a blueprint for a more secure, prosperous and just world.

Their key common focus, aside from globalisation itself, is the power of community. It is a sense of community within which – whether in the context of financial markets, climate change, international terrorism, or nuclear proliferation – our self-interest and our mutual interests are woven together.

The new power of community will transform domestic as well as international politics, because globalisation shrinks the distance between domestic and international issues. Indeed it often renders them identical: tackling terrorism in the USA means dealing with issues on the ground in the mountains of Afghanistan; bringing economic security to just one town in northern England means addressing the international machinery of global finance. The international has become domestic and the domestic international.

This does not mean that we should seek to stop the advance of globalisation – a hopeless task in any case. The goal suggested by the authors here is instead to channel and exploit globalisation for the good of all. A globalisation that only works for the few is wrong and deserves to fail. But by following the principles that have served liberal democracies well at home – that power, wealth and opportunity must be in the hands of the many, not the few – we can make globalisation a force for international good.

That is easier said than done: such a new international order will demand fresh thinking as well as courage. This book is a timely contribution to that debate.

London, March 2002

Introduction:
The Contours of a World Community

Mark Leonard

Shocks create the backdrop against which histories are played out. The events themselves may be haunting, but it is the choices we make afterwards which define their legacy. The balance of power and the principle of non-intervention were reactions to the murderous 30 Years War which had seen the Holy Roman Empire's power rise unchecked. The quest for peace and European Union came out of the World War II realisation that the balance of power was unsustainable in an age of nuclear weapons. Both these events show that even the most horrendous tragedies are pregnant with possibilities.

But the opportunities are not always seized, and failure to grasp a changed environment and so respond to it can be equally defining. The fall of the Berlin Wall was just such a missed chance. The defeat of Communism was seen as victory itself: a vindication of the structures and institutions that were in place rather than a challenge to reinvent them. The goal of Bush Senior's 'new world order', despite the rhetoric, was above all about stability – supporting discredited regimes in Yugoslavia and Somalia and leaving Saddam Hussein in power at the same time as preaching the virtues of liberal democracy. The contrast of this preservation of the status quo with the institutional creativity and long-sighted investments that followed World War II could not be starker.

Bin Laden is an aftershock of the mistakes made after 1989. Not in the simple sense that he was sustained by the West as part of the Cold War effort – but in the deeper sense that the West combined triumphalism with a failure to deliver change. Today there is a real opportunity to put this right and face up to the failures of a decade ago, but there is a danger of yet again proclaiming a new world while trying to preserve the status quo. The Cold War dichotomy of freedom versus communism has been replaced with a new organising principle: order versus disorder. The positive lesson to be taken out of this, which Jack Straw develops in his essay, is that the chaos of failed states can be more damaging and destructive than the overweening ambitions of powerful states. But the solution has sometimes been a mission to turn states into containers of problems – plugging the holes through which they seep rather than tackling their causes. The global crackdown on terror has been used as an excuse in many states for aggressive action to maintain their monopoly of violence and suppress dissent.

The age where states could act as containers is over. Anyone can board a plane with a bomb in their shoe or launch a biological attack regardless of where they are based. The fact that they can happen anywhere in the world means that all places take on an existence that is independent of their global economic and military 'significance'. This is why the very talk of order goes against the grain of a world that is facing unprecedented risks, uncertainties and changes which threaten all regardless of where they live or how privileged they are. Rather than trying to re-erect borders between us as a guarantee of order, we must find new ways of living together. What is needed is not a rigid world order but a set of rules and institutions to govern increasingly fluid relationships between states, citizens, companies and NGOs. By definition each solution to non-state problems – from pitting networks of police and intelligence against networks of criminals to working with NGOs to promote our values across borders – further weakens the traditional nation state.

Using power to prevent political change also creates difficulties. Propping up unpopular regimes and encouraging violent suppression of dissidents will create a backlash in the long-term. The Iranian Shah, Saddam Hussein, Slobodan Milosevic, Boris Yeltsin, Yasser Arafat are all leaders that the West supported – in the face of popular opposition – in order to maintain stability. Not all of these situations have ended in violent chaos but the West's association with them has discredited not only the countries involved but the idea of liberal democracy itself. That is why we must do what was left undone in 1989, and try to build a constituency for liberal democracy among citizens themselves.

This means that we need to think of a different kind of relationship between the community of states and the community of citizens and grapple with some of the necessary tensions between them. It is true that the rights of citizens will depend on the community of states making them real. But if short-term realpolitik is not guided by the values of democratic citizens it will not deliver security in the long-term. It is important that we start with the constraints of the real world – but we need to try to transcend them and connect the existing community of states with our aspirations for a community of citizens. Unless we do this, we will find that the real legacy of 1989 is a world where order clashes with justice and so leads inevitably to catastrophes like 11 September. This idea of a world community is a project to strive towards over decades – not something you can simply declare. The point is not to set out a single blueprint but to start a process of debate and negotiation which will hopefully result in a shared agenda.

Re-Ordering the World seeks to make a contribution to this debate. By bringing together thoughtful essays by international statesmen and agenda-setting proposals by some of the most creative thinkers in international affairs, this collection maps out the parameters of an exciting political project and explores the questions of security, values, and legitimacy that underlie this challenge. 11 September offers new hope in achieving this: not just because it highlights the problem, but because the response to it demonstrated the possibility of a global community.

Building a Community of States

Power without legitimacy cannot survive in the long-term. Realists in the United States – relying on their enormous military and economic power – claim that a lack of legitimacy does not stop the US from doing anything that it wants to do. It is powerful enough simply to assert its will and demand that others follow. Even if this were true (which despite American preponderance is unlikely) there will be much higher transaction costs if the US has to impose its will on others rather than rely on their sense that it is in their interests to collaborate.

Joseph Nye's piece in this volume shows the importance of 'soft power' – the idea of changing peoples' preferences over time so that they actually want what you want (what others have called the power of attraction rather than coercion). The differences in how the EU and US have dealt with their neighbours are illustrative. The threats are similar – drug trafficking, large flows of migrants across hard to police borders, trans-national criminal networks – but the responses could not be more different. The European response has been to hold out the possibility of integration (into the EU and into NATO) to the countries and so attempt to bring these countries closer to the political norms and institutional practices of the EU. The US has relied more heavily on swift military interventions where necessary to ensure its interests. One telling contrast is that between the EU's willingness to become deeply involved in the reconstruction of Serbia, and offer support and encouragement to its desire to be 'rehabilitated' as a European state, and the US's approach to Colombia. Colombia is offered no hope of closer integration with the US through multilateral institutions or structural funds, only the temporary 'assistance' of US military training missions, military aid and the raw freedom of the North American market.[1] While America values stability above all else, Europe has been about helping countries change. A growing number of satellite states have been given the incentives and assistance to develop and embrace modernity – to become what Robert Cooper's contribution to this volume would term a 'postmodern' state.

A rules-based community of states, like any other one, ultimately needs to be underpinned by credible force – good intentions without power lead to the shame of Sarajevo, and to the charge of hypocrisy against a West which proclaims values but is not prepared to risk anything to make them prevail. The hard truth is that the 'European project' of creating an international community will continue to depend heavily on American power in order to have any hope of subsisting. This will mean that its legitimacy will remain umbillically linked to America's standing in the world.

But there is little hope of persuading America to become a European power. In the immediate aftermath of 11 September people claimed that it had learned multilateralism, but it is now clear that America has only learned the frustrations of multilateralism – regarding even NATO as a terminally bureaucratic institution. Opposition to multilateralism runs deeper than any particular policies or interests – it is existential according Francis Fukuyama: "The US and Europe come at international law from such different angles. Every country in Europe has been busy divesting itself of sovereignty with the Euro and Maastricht. Americans still have an abiding belief in American exceptionalism and sovereignty. The American government still thinks that sources of legitimacy are national and that there are no higher sources of legitimacy. The traditional concern is that a lot of international law has been made by governments which are less democratic than the US".

Each fresh American onslaught on the painfully extracted advances of the late 20th century – from the International Criminal Court and Kyoto to the WTO and Chemical and Biological Weapons Convention – further risks unpicking the fabric of the international community. It signals to the rest of the world that there can be one rule for the strong and another for the weak. Furthermore, it creates perverse incentives to develop nuclear weapons – as India and Pakistan have done – in order to avoid the bullying censure endured by the rest of the world.

This creates a real dilemma for European countries. Standing aside with our principles intact while the US acts in a unilateral way could have an even more corrosive effect on liberal internationalism than explaining and supporting their actions. Tony Blair is accused by the left of simply supplying a multilateral fig-leaf for US actions, but the alternative may be no international legitimacy at all. For if the American administration remains unintertested in framing its actions in ways that appeal to wider audiences, it is vital that someone else takes on this role.

The European perception that this makes Blair simply cheerleader-in-chief is simplistic. Europe must pursue a three-pronged strategy: as well as an ambassadorial role and consultations on how to implement strategy, Europe must supply humanitarian assistance in the reconstruction of societies after military interventions. Some British diplomats and soldiers may bridle at a role that could be caricatured as international social work. But, as Malcolm Chalmers argues, prevention and reconstruction is the vital part of the jigsaw which is not on the American agenda. In many ways Europe's role in building global community mirrors Germany's role in the development of the European Union. While France and Britain have asserted the national interest and bristled at the idea of becoming net contributors to the EU, Germany until now has made a long-term investment and quietly paid for the EU's development, smoothing the disagreements between its more nationalistic fellow member states.

A Community of Citizens

The use of military power is important, but there is a danger of losing the battle for public opinion. Increasingly the external behaviour of states is a reflection of their internal politics, and as several authors point out in this book, liberal democracy is under threat at a popular level (see the contributions to this volume Fred Halliday, Kanan Makiya, and Fareed Zakaria). Many of the roots for this too can be traced to the end of the Cold War. People's hatred of the communist regime in Russia has translated into an even greater distrust of liberal democracy and capitalism. It is not just the palpable deteriotaion in quality of life but a rejection of the values they were so desperate to embrace: the World Values Survey showed that less than half of the Russian population is committed to democracy. Of course, it is not just Russia, many developing countries have balanced their budgets, cut subsidies, welcomed foreign investment and dropped their tariff barriers and been repaid with poverty, turmoil, and instability. The fact that we are increasingly subject to the same cultural flows and aspirations – but that our experience is so different – is creating new tensions. The ideas, culture, and norms that have travelled with goods have had a paradoxical effect on world order. In many parts of the world, people have taken liberal democracy's promise at face value and been bitterly disappointed. The willingness of the international community to let countries like Argentina go bust is seen side by side with the double standards and hypocrisy of a West that refuses to practice the free trade they preach. A new generation of populist leaders such as Chavez in Venezuela are taking advantage of popular discontent with globalisation to entrench their political base. Post-Communism has failed in the same way that post-colonialism failed before it.

Francis Fukuyama is right to claim that we have reached the end of history in the sense that there is no coherent alternative to liberal democracy: it is not to be found on the streets of Seattle, Genoa, North Korea or in the caves of Afghanistan. But liberal democracy appears to be winning only because there is no alternative. In fact, it is the very absence of an alternative which drives so many people to their violent rejection of Western values and the Western way of life. Saying that liberal democracy is inevitable is not just a mistake because history shows that nothing is inevitable or irreversible but because it alienates Southern countries and creates fanatical enemies. It lends weight to feelings of invulnerability in the US and other northern countries, makes them complacent, and means that precautions are not taken to ensure that globalisation both delivers and is seen to deliver for societies undergoing painful transitions. Above all the claim that liberal democracy is inevitable hollows out our idea of a political sphere and denies the possibilities of purposeful politics.

The challenge is to develop popular legitimacy for the values of liberal democracy. Whereas in the past it was seen as a technocratic project – run by economists to appeal to the Westernised elites – it must become a political movement capable of mobilizing the public at large. This encompasses the arguments made by David Held and Mary Kaldor in this volume for the creation of a global sphere of justice to mirror the globalisation of finance – but it must go further as an attempt to create a community of global feeling.

After 11 September governments started to focus on the depth of anti-Western feeling around the world. There was a realisation that the biggest dangers to the coalition were not the weapons of the Taliban but the fact that public support for key allies could have collapsed at any time. The delicate balancing act between domestic constituencies and international public opinion – played out across different time-zones – illustrated the difficulties of winning and maintaining support. But there is a difference between short-term propaganda efforts and long-term relationship building. An official in the White House confessed to me, "We haven't made any attempts to communicate with ordinary Arabs unless we are bombing them or imposing sanctions on them – I wouldn't like us if I were them". The Americans know this better than anyone else. The collapse of Communism was arguably brought about because people on the other side of the Iron Curtain were prepared to die for a Western way of life which they glimpsed on their television screens. The Americans spent billions of dollars on getting their messages to Communist citizens. Yet, today, the very fact that the United States is involved in an initiative is enough to attract suspicion to it.

Imagining a Global Community

The danger is that the campaign in Afghanistan will simply confirm everyone's original thinking. For the American right, as well as proving that 'non-state' threats could be reduced to cryptic 'state-threats', it showed the importance of military superiority and realpolitik in the regional diplomacy that followed. On the European left, the images of jubilation from Afghans who were once again able to go to school, shave, listen to music, or lead a free life, allowed people to see it as a humanitarian intervention on the same mould as Kosovo or Sierra Leone. This allowed European Governments to avoid facing up to the need for effective military resources for self-defence.

But, as Ulrich Beck argues, there is something profound in the global reaction to the attacks: the emergence of a global consciousness which spreads from an elite of political leaders, businessmen and NGOs to a new underclass of migrant workers, unskilled-labourers whose livelihoods are threatened by cheap global competition and Iranian feminists demanding new rights in their own countries.

There has been a global consciousness before but it was always about national destinies: the vision of one or other competing sovereign state growing to global proportions. No one seriously thought about a global community with rights and responsibilities. As Amartya Sen demonstrates in his piece, any division of human beings into concrete (and opposing) boxes will not reflect the complexity of contemporary life.

Academics have shown us that the best way to understand the emergence of nationalism is to understand each nation state as an 'imagined community'. This means that to change the world we need to be able to imagine it. The most important thing is not necessarily the reality, but what people think they are doing.[2] This was encapsulated by the anthropolgist W I Thomas in his famous theorem: "If men define situations as real, they are real in their consequences."

The barriers to overcome are overwhelming and the tensions between the world community of states and the world community of citizens are real. There are many more governments around the world who are opposed to this agenda than support it. But there are the beginnings of a new consensus emerging, and if they are backed up by political will the world community could be within our grasp.

Mark Leonard is Director of The Foreign Policy Centre.

[1] Malcolm Chalmers makes this point eloquently in *A Transatlantic New Deal: what Europe should pay to promote US engagement* (London: The Foreign Policy Centre, 2001). Available online at www.fpc.org.uk/reports.

[2] Benedict Anderson, *Imagined Communities: reflections on the origin and spread of nationalism. (London: Verso, 1983)*

PART I
Power in the Modern World

1 Hard and Soft Power in a Global Information Age

Joseph Nye

The nature of power in world politics is changing. Power is the ability to effect the outcomes you want, and, if necessary, to change the behaviour of others to make this happen. In the 21st century, under the influence of the information revolution and globalisation, the sources and distribution of power are being transformed in a profound way. Non-state actors have gained greater power and, as a result, more activities are outside the control of even the most powerful states. The recent terrorist attacks on New York and Washington dramatised this change. 11 September 2001 also showed us that there is no alternative to mobilising international coalitions and building institutions to address shared threats and challenges. More than ever before, the United States – and others – will have to include global interests in formulating their own national interests. No country today is great enough to solve the problem of global terrorism alone.

The Role of Force

Traditionally, the test of a great power was 'strength for war'.[1] War was the ultimate game in which the cards of international politics were played and estimates of relative power were proven. Over the centuries, as technologies evolved, the sources of power have shifted. Today, the foundations of power have been moving away from the emphasis on military force and conquest. Paradoxically, nuclear weapons were one of the causes. As we know from the history of the Cold War, nuclear weapons proved so awesome and destructive that they became muscle-bound – too costly to use except, theoretically, in the most extreme circumstances.[2] A second important change was the rise of nationalism, which has made it more difficult for empires to rule over awakened populations. In the 19th century, a few adventurers conquered most of

Africa with a handful of soldiers, and Britain ruled India with a colonial force that was a tiny fraction of the indigenous population. Today, colonial rule is not only widely condemned but far too costly, as both Cold War superpowers discovered in Vietnam and Afghanistan. The collapse of the Soviet empire followed the end of the European empires by a matter of decades.

A third important cause is social change inside great powers. Post-industrial societies are focused on welfare rather than glory, and they loathe high casualties, except when survival is at stake. This does not mean that they will not use force, even when casualties are expected – witness the 1991 Gulf War and US and allied military involvement in Afghanistan today. But the absence of a warrior ethic in modern democracies means that the use of force requires an elaborate moral justification to ensure popular support. Roughly speaking, there are three types of countries in the world today: poor, weak pre-industrial states, which are often the chaotic remnants of collapsed empires; modernising industrial states such as India or China; and the post-industrial societies that prevail in Europe, North America, and Japan. The use of force is common in the first type of country, still accepted in the second, but less tolerated in the third. In the words of British diplomat Robert Cooper, "a large number of the most powerful states no longer want to fight or conquer".[3] War remains possible, but it is much less acceptable now than it was a century or even half a century ago.[4]

Finally, for most of today's great powers, the use of force would jeopardise their economic objectives. Even non-democratic countries that feel fewer popular moral constraints on the use of force have to consider its effects on their economic objectives. As Thomas Friedman has put it, countries are disciplined by an "electronic herd" of investors who control their access to capital in a globalised economy.[5]

None of this is to suggest that military force plays no role in international politics today. For one thing, the information revolution has yet to transform most of the world. Many states are unconstrained by democratic social forces, as Kuwait learned from its neighbour Iraq, and terrorist groups pay little heed to the normal constraints of liberal societies. Civil wars are rife in many parts of the world where collapsed empires left power vacuums. Moreover, throughout history, the rise of new great powers has been accompanied by anxieties that have sometimes precipitated military crises. In Thucydides' immortal description, the Peloponnesian War in ancient Greece was caused by the rise to power of Athens and the fear it created in Sparta.[6] World War I owed much to the rise of the Kaiser's Germany and the fear this created in Britain.[7] Some foretell a similar dynamic in this century arising from the rise of China and the fear it creates in the United States.

Geo-economics has not replaced geopolitics, although in the early 21st century there has clearly been a blurring of the traditional boundaries between the two. To ignore the role of force and the centrality of security would be like ignoring oxygen. Under normal circumstances, oxygen is plentiful and we pay it little attention. But once those conditions change and we begin to miss it, we can focus on nothing else.[8] Even in those areas where the direct employment of force falls out of use among countries – for instance, within western Europe or between the United States and Japan – non-state actors such as terrorists may use force. With that said, economic power *has* become more important than in the past, both because of the relative increase in the costliness of force and because economic objectives loom larger in the values of post-industrial societies.[9] In a world of economic globalisation, all countries are to some extent dependent on market forces beyond their direct control.

Soft Power

Military power and economic power are both examples of hard command power that can be used to induce others to change their position. Hard power can rest on inducements (carrots) or threats (sticks). But there is also an indirect way to exercise power. A country may obtain the outcomes it wants in world politics because other countries want to follow it, admiring its values, emulating its example, aspiring to its level of prosperity and openness. In this sense, it is just as important to set the agenda in world politics and attract others as it is to force them to change through the threat or use of military or economic weapons. This aspect of power getting others to want what you want I call soft power.[10] It co-opts people rather than coerces them.

Soft power rests on the ability to set the political agenda in a way that shapes the preferences of others. At the personal level, wise parents know that if they have brought up their children with the right beliefs and values, their power will be greater and will last longer than if they have relied only on spankings, cutting off allowances, or taking away the car keys. Similarly, political leaders and thinkers such as Antonio Gramsci have long understood the power that comes from setting the agenda and determining the framework of a debate. The ability to establish preferences tends to be associated with intangible power resources such as an attractive culture, ideology, and institutions. If I can get you to want to do what I want, then I do not have to force you to do what you do not want to do. If a country represents values that others want to follow, it will cost us less to lead. Soft power is not merely the same as influence, though it is one source of influence. After all, I can also influence you by threats or rewards. Soft power is also more than persuasion or the ability to move people by argument. It is the ability to entice and attract. And attraction often leads to acquiescence or imitation.

Of course, hard and soft power are related and can reinforce each other. Both are aspects of the ability to achieve our purposes by affecting the behaviour of others. Sometimes the same power resources can affect the entire spectrum of behaviour from coercion to attraction.[11] A country that suffers economic and military decline is likely to lose its ability to shape the international agenda as well as its attractiveness. And some countries may be attracted to others with hard power by the myth of invincibility or inevitability. Both Hitler and Stalin tried to develop such myths. Hard power can also be used to establish empires and institutions that set the agenda for smaller states – witness Soviet rule over the countries of eastern Europe.

But soft power is not simply the reflection of hard power. The Vatican did not lose its soft power when it lost the Papal States in Italy in the 19th century. Conversely, the Soviet Union lost much of its soft power after it invaded Hungary and Czechoslovakia, even though its economic and military resources continued to grow. Imperious policies that utilised Soviet hard power actually undercut its soft power. And some countries such as Canada, the Netherlands, and the Scandinavian states have political clout that is greater than their military and economic weight, because of the incorporation of attractive causes such as economic aid or peacekeeping into their definitions of national interest.

Soft power in an information age

The countries that are likely to gain soft power in an information age are (1) those whose dominant culture and ideas are closer to prevailing global norms (which now emphasise liberalism, pluralism, and autonomy), (2) those with the most access to multiple channels of communication and thus more influence over how issues are framed, and (3) those whose credibility is enhanced by their domestic and international performance. These dimensions of power in an information age suggest the growing importance of soft power in the mix of power resources, and a strong advantage to the United States and Europe.

Soft power is not brand new, nor was the United States the first government to try to utilise its culture to create soft power. After its defeat in the Franco-Prussian War, the French government sought to repair the nation's shattered prestige by promoting its language and literature through the Alliance Française, created in 1883. "The projection of French culture abroad thus became a significant component of French diplomacy."[12] Italy, Germany, and others soon followed suit. The advent of radio in the 1920s led many governments into the area of foreign language broadcasting, and in the 1930s, Nazi Germany perfected the propaganda film.

The American government was a latecomer to the idea of using American culture for the purposes of diplomacy. It established a Committee on Public Information during World War I but abolished it with the return of peace. By the late 1930s, the Roosevelt administration became convinced that "America's security depended on its ability to speak to and to win the support of people in other countries". With World War II and the Cold War, the government became more active, with official efforts such as the United States Information Agency, the Voice of America, the Fulbright programme, American libraries, lectures, and other programmes. But much soft power arises from social forces outside government control. Even before the Cold War, "American corporate and advertising executives, as well as the heads of Hollywood studios, were selling not only their products but also America's culture and values, the secrets of its success, to the rest of the world".[13] Soft power is created partly by governments and partly in spite of them.

A decade ago some observers thought the close collaboration of government and industry in Japan would give it a lead in soft power in the information age. Japan could develop an ability to manipulate perceptions worldwide instantaneously and "destroy those that impede Japanese economic prosperity and cultural acceptance".[14] When Matsushita purchased MCA, its president said that movies critical of Japan would not be produced.[15] Japanese media tried to break into world markets, and the government-owned NHK network began satellite broadcasts in English. The venture failed, however, as NHK's reports seemed to lag behind those of commercial news organisations, and the network had to rely on CNN and ABC.[16] This does not mean that Japan lacks soft power. On the contrary, its pop culture has great appeal to teenagers in Asia.[17] But Japan's culture remains much more inward-oriented than that of the United States.

To be sure, there are areas, such as the Middle East, where ambivalence about, or outright opposition to, American culture limits its soft power. All television in the Arab world used to be state-run until tiny Qatar allowed a new station, Al-Jazeera, to broadcast freely, and it proved wildly popular in the Middle East.[18] Its uncensored images, ranging from Osama bin Laden to Tony Blair, have had a powerful political influence. Bin Laden's ability to project a Robin Hood image enhanced his soft power with some Muslims around the globe. As an Arab journalist described the situation earlier, "Al-Jazeera has been for this intifada what CNN was to the Gulf War".[19] In the eyes of Islamic fundamentalists, the openness of western culture is repulsive. But for much of the world, including many moderates and young people, our culture still attracts. To the extent that official policies at home and abroad are consistent with democracy, human rights, openness, and respect for the opinions of others, the United States and Europe will benefit from the trends of this global information age, although pockets of fundamentalism will persist and react in some countries.

Conclusion

Power in the global information age is becoming less tangible and less coercive, particularly among advanced countries, but most of the world does not consist of post-industrial societies, and that limits the transformation of power. Much of Africa and the Middle East remains locked in pre-industrial agricultural societies with weak institutions and authoritarian rulers. Other countries, such as China, India, and Brazil, are industrial economies analogous to parts of the West in the mid-20th century.[20] In such a variegated world, all three sources of power – military, economic, and soft – remain relevant, although to different degrees in different relationships. However, if current economic and social trends continue, leadership in the information revolution and soft power will become more important in the mix.

Joseph Nye is dean of the Kennedy School of Government at Harvard University. This essay draws upon his new book, *The Paradox of American Power* (Oxford University Press, 2002).

[1] A. J. Taylor, *The Struggle for Mastery in Europe, 1848–1918* (Oxford: Oxford University Press, 1954), xxix.

[2] Whether this would change with the proliferation of nuclear weapons to more states is hotly debated among theorists. Deterrence should work with most states, but the prospects of accident and loss of control would increase. For my views, see Joseph S. Nye Jr., *Nuclear Ethics* (New York: Free Press, 1986).

[3] Robert Cooper, *The Postmodern State and the World Order* (London: Demos / The Foreign Policy Centre, 2000), 22.

[4] John Mueller, *Retreat from Doomsday: The Obsolescence of Major War* (New York: Basic Books, 1989).

[5] Thomas Friedman, *The Lexus and the Olive Tree: Understanding Globalization* (New York: Farrar, Straus and Giroux, 1999), chapter 6.

[6] Thucydides, *History of the Peloponnesian War*, trans. Rex Warner (London: Penguin, 1972), book I, chapter 1.

[7] And in turn, as industrialisation progressed and railroads were built, Germany feared the rise of Russia.

[8] Henry Kissinger portrays four international systems existing side by side: the West (and Western Hemisphere), marked by democratic peace; Asia, where strategic conflict is possible; the Middle East, marked by religious conflict; and Africa, where civil wars threaten weak postcolonial states. "America at the Apex", *The National Interest*, summer 2001, 14.

[9] Robert O. Keohane and Joseph S. Nye Jr., *Power and Interdependence*, 3rd ed. (New York: Longman, 2000), chapter 1.

[10] For a more detailed discussion, see Joseph S. Nye Jr., *Bound to Lead: The Changing Nature of American Power* (New York: Basic Books, 1990), chapter 2. This builds on what Peter Bachrach and Morton Baratz called the "second face of power" in "Decisions and Nondecisions: An Analytical Framework," *American Political Science Review*, September 1963, 632–42.

[11] The distinction between hard and soft power is one of degree, both in the nature of the behaviour and in the tangibility of the resources. Both are aspects of the ability to achieve one's purposes by affecting the behaviour of others. Command power – the ability to change what others do – can rest on coercion or inducement. Co-optive power – the ability to shape what others want – can rest on the attractiveness of one's culture and ideology or the ability to manipulate the agenda of political choices in a manner that makes actors fail to express some preferences because they seem to be too unrealistic. The forms of behaviour between command and co-optive power range along a continuum: command power, coercion, inducement, agenda setting, attraction, co-optive power. Soft power resources tend to be associated with co-optive power behaviour, whereas hard power resources are usually associated with command behaviour. But the relationship is imperfect. For example, countries may be attracted to others with command power by myths of invincibility, and command power may sometimes be used to establish institutions that later become regarded as legitimate. But the general association is strong enough to allow the useful shorthand reference to hard and soft power.

[12] Richard Pells, *Not Like Us* (New York: Basic Books, 1997), 31–32.

[13] Ibid., 33, xiii.

[14] Jerome C. Glenn, 'Japan: Cultural Power of the Future,' *Nikkei Weekly*, December 7, 1992, 7.

[15] 'Multinational Movies: Questions on Politics,' *New York Times*, November 27, 1990, D7.

[16] 'Japanese News Media Join Export Drive,' *International Herald Tribune*, May 10, 1991; David Sanger, 'NHK of Japan Ends Plan for Global News Service,' *New York Times*, December 9, 1991.

[17] Calvin Sims, 'Japan Beckons and East Asia's Youth Fall in Love,' *New York Times*, December 5, 1999, A3; 'Advance of the Amazonesu,' *The Economist*, July 22, 2000, 61.

[18] Mark Huband, 'Egypt Tries to Tempt Back Broadcasters,' *Financial Times* (London), March 7, 2000, 14.

[19] John Kifner, 'Tale of Two Uprisings,' *New York Times*, November 18, 2000, A6.

[20] See Cooper, *Postmodern State*, and Daniel Bell, *The Coming of Post-Industrial Society* (New York: Basic Books, 1999) [original 1973].

2   The Post-Modern State

Robert Cooper

In 1989 the political systems of three centuries came to an end in Europe: the balance of power and the imperial urge. That year marked not just the end of the Cold War, but also, and more significantly, the end of a state system in Europe which dated from the Thirty Years War. 11 September showed us one of the implications of the change.

To understand the present, we must first understand the past, for the past is still with us. International order used to be based either on hegemony or on balance. Hegemony came first. In the ancient world, order meant empire. Those within the empire had order, culture and civilisation. Outside it lay barbarians, chaos and disorder. The image of peace and order through a single hegemonic power centre has remained strong ever since. Empires, however, are ill-designed for promoting change. Holding the empire together – and it is the essence of empires that they are diverse – usually requires an authoritarian political style; innovation, especially in society and politics, would lead to instability. Historically, empires have generally been static.

In Europe, a middle way was found between the stasis of chaos and the stasis of empire, namely the small state. The small state succeeded in establishing sovereignty, but only within a geographically limited jurisdiction. Thus domestic order was purchased at the price of international anarchy. The competition between the small states of Europe was a source of progress, but the system was also constantly threatened by a relapse into chaos on one side and by the hegemony of a single power on the other. The solution to this was the balance of power, a system of counter-balancing alliances which became seen as the condition of liberty in Europe. Coalitions were successfully put together to thwart the hegemonic ambitions firstly of Spain, then of France, and finally of Germany.

But the balance of power system too had an inherent instability, the ever-present risk of war, and it was this that eventually caused it to collapse. German unification in 1871 created a state too powerful to be balanced by any European alliance; technological changes raised the costs of war to an unbearable level; and the development of mass society and democratic politics rendered impossible the amoral calculating mindset necessary to make the balance of power system function. Nevertheless, in the absence of any obvious alternative it persisted, and what emerged in 1945 was not so much a new system as the culmination of the old one. The old multi-lateral balance of power in Europe became a bilateral balance of terror worldwide, a final simplification of the balance of power. But it was not built to last. The balance of power never suited the more universalist, moralist spirit of the late 20th century.

The second half of the 20th century saw not just the end of the balance of power but also the waning of the imperial urge: in some degree the two go together. A world that started the century divided among European empires finishes it with all or almost all of them gone: the Ottoman, German, Austrian, French, British and finally Soviet empires are now no more than a memory. This leaves us with two new types of state: first there are now states – often former colonies – where in some sense the state has almost ceased to exist: a 'premodern' zone where the state has failed and a Hobbesian war of all against all is underway (countries such as Somalia and, until recently, Afghanistan). Second, there are the post-imperial, postmodern states that no longer think of security primarily in terms of conquest. And thirdly, of course there remain the traditional "modern" states that behave as states always have, following Machiavellian principles and *raison d'état* (one thinks of countries such as India, Pakistan and China).

The postmodern system in which we Europeans live does not rely on balance; nor does it emphasise sovereignty or the separation of domestic and foreign affairs. The European Union has become a highly-developed system for mutual interference in each other's domestic affairs, right down to beer and sausages. The CFE Treaty, under which parties to the treaty have to notify the location of their heavy weapons and allow inspections, subjects areas close to the core of sovereignty to international constraints. It is important to realise what an extraordinary revolution this is. It mirrors the paradox of the nuclear age: that in order to defend yourself, you had to be prepared to destroy yourself. The shared interest of European countries in avoiding a nuclear catastrophe has proved enough to overcome the normal strategic logic of distrust and concealment. Mutual vulnerability has become mutual transparency.

The main characteristics of the postmodern world are as follows:

- The breaking down of the distinction between domestic and foreign affairs
- Mutual interference in (traditional) domestic affairs and mutual surveillance
- The rejection of force for resolving disputes and the consequent codification of self enforced rules of behaviour
- The growing irrelevance of borders: this has come about both through the changing role of the state, but also through missiles, motor cars and satellites
- Security is based on transparency, mutual openness, interdependence and mutual vulnerability.

The conception of an international criminal court is a striking example of the postmodern breakdown of the distinction between domestic and foreign affairs. In the postmodern world, *raison d'état* and the amorality of Machiavelli's theories of statecraft, which defined international relations in the modern era, have been replaced by a moral consciousness that applies to international relations as well as to domestic affairs hence the renewed interest in what constitutes a just war.

While such a system does deal with the problems that made the balance of power unworkable, it does not entail the demise of the nation state. While economy, law-making and defence may be increasingly embedded in international frameworks, and the borders of territory may be less important, identity and democratic institutions remain primarily national. Thus traditional states will remain the fundamental unit of international relations for the foreseeable future, even though some of them may have ceased to behave in traditional ways.

What is the origin of this basic change in the state system? The fundamental point is that 'the world's grown honest'.[1] A large number of the most powerful states no longer want to fight or conquer. It is this that gives rise to both the pre-modern and postmodern worlds. Imperialism in the traditional sense is dead, at least among the western powers.

If this is true, it follows that we should not think of the EU or even NATO as the root cause of the half-century of peace we have enjoyed in western Europe. The basic fact is that western European countries no longer want to fight each other. NATO and the EU have, nevertheless, played an important role in reinforcing and sustaining this position. NATO's most valuable contribution has been the openness it has created. NATO was, and is, a massive intra-western confidence-building measure. It was NATO and the EU that provided the framework within which Germany could be reunited without posing a threat to the rest of Europe as its original unification had in 1871. Both give rise to thousands of meetings of ministers and officials, so that all those concerned with decisions involving war and peace know each other well. Compared with the past, this represents a quality and stability of political relations never known before.

The EU is the most developed example of a postmodern system. It represents security through transparency, and transparency through interdependence. The EU is more a transnational than a supra-national system, a voluntary association of states rather than the subordination of states to a central power. The dream of a European state is one left from a previous age. It rests on the assumption that nation states are fundamentally dangerous and that the only way to tame the anarchy of nations is to impose hegemony on them. But if the nation state is a problem then the super-state is certainly not a solution.

European states are not the only members of the postmodern world. Outside Europe, Canada is certainly a postmodern state; Japan is by inclination a postmodern state, but its location prevents it developing more fully in this direction. The USA is the more doubtful case since it is not clear that the US government or Congress accepts either the necessity or desirability of interdependence, or its corollaries of openness, mutual surveillance and mutual interference, to the same extent as most European governments now do. Elsewhere, what in Europe has become a reality is in many other parts of the world an aspiration. ASEAN, NAFTA, MERCOSUR and even OAU suggest at least the desire for a postmodern environment, and though this wish is unlikely to be realised quickly, imitation is undoubtedly easier than invention.

Within the postmodern world, there are no security threats in the traditional sense; that is to say, its members do not consider invading each other. Whereas in the modern world, following Clausewitz's dictum, war is an instrument of policy, in the postmodern world it is a sign of policy failure. But while the members of the postmodern world may not represent a danger to one another, both the modern and pre-modern zones pose threats. The threat from the modern world is the most familiar. Here, the classical state system, from which the postmodern world has only recently emerged, remains intact, and continues to operate by the principles of empire and the supremacy of national interest. If there is to be stability it will come from a balance among the aggressive forces. It is notable how few are the areas of the world where such a balance exists. And how sharp the risk is that in some areas there may soon be a nuclear element in the equation. The challenge to the postmodern world is to get used to the idea of double-standards. Among ourselves, we operate on the basis of laws and open co-operative security. But when dealing with more old-fashioned kinds of states outside the postmodern continent of Europe, we need to revert to the rougher methods of an earlier era – force, pre-emptive attack, deception, whatever is necessary to deal with those who still live in the 19th century world of "every state for itself". Among ourselves, we keep the law but when we are operating in the jungle, we must also use the laws of the jungle. In the prolonged period of peace in Europe, there has been a temptation to neglect our defences, both physical and psychological. This represents one of the great dangers of the postmodern state.

The challenge posed by the pre-modern world is a new one. The pre-modern world is a world of failed states. Here the state no longer fulfils Weber's criterion of having the monopoly on the legitimate use of force. Either it has lost legitimacy or it has lost the monopoly of the use of force; often the two go together. Examples of total collapse are relatively rare, but the number of countries at risk grows all the time. Some areas of the former Soviet Union are candidates, including Chechnya. All of the world's major drug-producing areas are part of the pre-modern world. Until recently there was no real sovereign authority in Afghanistan; nor is there in upcountry Burma or in some parts of South America, where drug barons threaten the state's monopoly on force. All over Africa countries are at risk. No area of the world is without its dangerous cases. In such areas chaos is the norm and war is a way of life. Insofar as there is a government it operates in a way similar to an organised crime syndicate.

The premodern state may be too weak even to secure its home territory, let alone pose a threat internationally, but it can provide a base for non-state actors who may represent a danger to the postmodern world. If non-state actors, notably drug, crime, or terrorist syndicates take to using pre-modern bases for attacks on the more orderly parts of the world, then the organised states may eventually have to respond. If they become too dangerous for established states to tolerate, it is possible to imagine a defensive imperialism. It is not going too far to view the West's response to Afghanistan in this light.

How should we deal with the pre-modern chaos? To become involved in a zone of chaos is risky; if the intervention is prolonged it may become unsustainable in public opinion; if the intervention is unsuccessful it may be damaging to the government that ordered it. But the risks of letting countries rot, as the West did Afghanistan, may be even greater.

What form should intervention take? The most logical way to deal with chaos, and the one most often employed in the past, is colonisation. But colonisation is unacceptable to postmodern states (and, as it happens, to some modern states too). It is precisely because of the death of imperialism that we are seeing the emergence of the pre-modern world. Empire and imperialism are words that have become terms of abuse in the postmodern world. Today, there are no colonial powers willing to take on the job, though the opportunities, perhaps even the need, for colonisation is as great as it ever was in the 19th century. Those left out of the global economy risk falling into a vicious circle. Weak government means disorder and that means falling investment. In the 1950s, South Korea had a lower GNP per head than Zambia; one has since achieved membership of the global economy, the other has not.

All the conditions for imperialism are there, but both the supply and demand for imperialism have dried up. And yet the weak still need the strong and the strong still need an orderly world. A world in which the efficient and well-governed export stability and liberty, and which is open for investment and growth – all of this seems eminently desirable.

What is needed then is a new kind of imperialism, one acceptable to a world of human rights and cosmopolitan values. We can already discern its outline: an imperialism which, like all imperialism, aims to bring order and organisation but which rests today on the voluntary principle.

Postmodern imperialism takes two forms. First there is the voluntary imperialism of the global economy. This is usually operated by an international consortium through international financial institutions such as the IMF and the World Bank – it is characteristic of the new imperialism that it is multilateral. These institutions provide help to states wishing to find their way back into the global economy and into the virtuous circle of investment and prosperity. In return they make demands which, they hope, address the political and economic failures that have contributed to the original need for assistance. Aid theory today increasingly emphasises governance. If states wish to benefit, they must open themselves up to the interference of international organisations and foreign states (just as, for different reasons, the postmodern world has also opened itself up).

The second form of postmodern imperialism might be called the imperialism of neighbours. Instability in your neighbourhood poses threats which no state can ignore. Misgovernment, ethnic violence and crime in the Balkans poses a threat to Europe. The response has been to create something like a voluntary UN protectorate in Bosnia and Kosovo. It is no surprise that in both cases the High Representative is European. Europe provides most of the aid that keeps Bosnia and Kosovo running and most of the soldiers (though the US presence is an indispensable stabilising factor). In a further unprecedented move, the EU has offered unilateral free-market access to all the countries of the former Yugoslavia for all products including most agricultural produce. It is not just soldiers that come from the international community; it is police, judges, prison officers, central bankers and others. Elections are organised and monitored by the Organisation for Security and Cooperation in Europe (OSCE). Local police are financed and trained by the UN. As auxiliaries to this effort – in many areas indispensable to it – are over 100 NGOs.

One additional point needs to be made. It is dangerous if a neighbouring state is taken over in some way by organised or disorganised crime – which is what state collapse usually amounts to. But Osama bin Laden has now demonstrated for those who had not already realised, that today all the world is, potentially at least, our neighbour.

The Balkans are a special case. Elsewhere in central and eastern Europe the EU is engaged in a programme which will eventually lead to massive enlargement. In the past empires have imposed their laws and systems of government; in this case no-one is imposing anything. Instead, a voluntary movement of self-imposition is taking place. While you are a candidate for EU membership you have to accept what is given – a whole mass of laws and regulations as subject countries once did. But the prize is that once you are inside you will have a voice in the commonwealth. If this process is a kind of voluntary imperialism, the end state might be described as a co-operative empire. 'Commonwealth' might indeed not be a bad name.

The postmodern EU offers a vision of co-operative empire, a common liberty and a common security without the ethnic domination and centralised absolutism to which past empires have been subject, but also without the ethnic exclusiveness that is the hallmark of the nation state – inappropriate in an era without borders and unworkable in regions such as the Balkans. A co-operative empire might be the domestic political framework that best matches the altered substance of the postmodern state: a framework in which each has a share in the government, in which no single country dominates and in which the governing principles are not ethnic but legal. The lightest of touches will be required from the centre; the 'imperial bureaucracy' must be under control, accountable, and the servant, not the master, of the commonwealth. Such an institution must be as dedicated to liberty and democracy as its constituent parts. Like Rome, this commonwealth would provide its citizens with some of its laws, some coins and the occasional road.

That perhaps is the vision. Can it be realised? Only time will tell. The question is how much time there may be. In the modern world the secret race to acquire nuclear weapons goes on. In the pre-modern world the interests of organised crime – including international terrorism – grow greater and faster than the state. There may not be much time left.

Robert Cooper is a senior serving British diplomat.

[1] *Hamlet*, Act II, scene ii, 235. See also line 236.

3   The Power of Terror

Mary Kaldor

President Bush is perhaps right to call what happened on 11 September a 'new kind of war'. But this is not the first 'new war', although it is more spectacular and more global than ever before and, for the first time, involves large-scale loss of American lives. Wars of this type have taken place in Africa, the Middle East, the Balkans and Central Asia, especially in the past decade. And there are lessons to be learned, which are relevant to the new 'new war'.

These new wars have to be understood in the context of globalisation. They are quite different from what we might call 'old wars' – wars between states, in which the aim is to inflict maximum damage on an enemy, and in which the decisive encounter is battle. 'Old wars' were inextricably linked to the rise of the state and the monopolisation of organised violence within a given territory. The Cold War can be regarded as the last great global clash between states; it marked the end of an era when the ultimate threat of war between states determined international relations and when the idea of war disciplined and polarised domestic politics. Nowadays, as 11 September demonstrated only too graphically, we live in an interdependent world, where we cannot maintain security merely through the protection of borders, where states no longer control what happens within their borders and where old-fashioned war between states has become too destructive to be contemplated. Today states are still important, but they function in a world shaped less by military power than by complex political processes involving international institutions, multinational corporations, citizens' groups and indeed fundamentalists and terrorists.

The end of old-fashioned war between states does not mean the end of violence. Instead, we are witnessing the rise of new types of violence, which we could call 'new wars'. The new wars involve transnational networks, which include both state and non-state actors – mercenary groups, warlords, as well as parts of state apparatuses. They are generally held together through shared political ideologies, which tend to consist of exclusive claims to power and resources in the name of religion or ethnicity. These networks provide organising frameworks, through which ideas, money, arms, volunteers and mercenaries are organised. They flourish in those areas of the world where states have imploded as a consequence of the impact of globalisation on formerly closed authoritarian systems. It is the 'black holes' where conflict has a long or bloody history, like Afghanistan, Chechnya, or Bosnia or Somalia, that provide a focal point for these networks.

In the new wars, the goal is not military victory; it is political mobilisation. In old-fashioned wars the aim of war was, to quote Clausewitz, "to compel an opponent to fulfil our will", and people were mobilised to participate in the war effort – to join the army or to produce weapons and uniforms. In the new wars, mobilising people is the aim of the war effort. The point of the violence is not so much directed against the enemy; rather the aim is to expand the networks of extremism. In the new wars, battles are rare and violence is directed against civilians. Indeed, the warring parties use techniques of terror, ethnic cleansing or genocide as deliberate war strategies. Violations of humanitarian and human rights law are not a side-effect of war but the central methodology of new wars.

The strategy is to gain political power through sowing fear and hatred, to create a climate of terror, to eliminate moderate voices and to defeat tolerance. The political ideologies of exclusive nationalism or religious communalism are generated through violence. It is generally assumed that extreme ideologies, based on exclusive identities – Serb nationalism, for example, or fundamentalist Islam – are the cause of war. Rather, the spread and strengthening of these ideologies are the consequence of war. 'The war had to be so bloody', Bosnians will tell you 'because we did not hate each other; we had to be taught to hate each other.

The goals of the new wars are not only political; economic power is important as well. These networks flourish in states where systems of taxation have collapsed and where little new wealth is being created. The wars destroy physical infrastructure, cut off trade and create a climate of insecurity that prohibits investment. Instead, the networks establish an alternative political economy – the globalised informal economy that depends on criminal and semi-legal activities. They raise money through loot and plunder, through illegal trading in drugs, illegal immigrants, cigarettes and alcohol, through 'taxing' humanitarian assistance, through support from sympathetic states and through remittances from members of the networks. All of these types of economic activity are predatory and depend on an atmosphere of insecurity.

The new wars are very difficult to contain and very difficult to end. They spread through refugees and displaced persons, through criminal networks, and through the extremist viruses they germinate. We can observe growing clusters of warfare in Africa, the Middle East, Central Asia or the Caucasus. The wars represent a defeat for democratic politics, and each bout of warfare strengthens those with a vested political and economic interest in continued violence. The areas where conflicts have lasted longest have generated cultures of violence, as in the jihad culture taught in religious schools in Pakistan and Afghanistan or among the Tamils of Sri Lanka, where young children are taught to be martyrs and where killing is understood as an offering to God. In the instructions found in the car of the hijackers in Boston's Logan Airport, it is written: "If God grants any one of you a slaughter, you should perform it as an offering on behalf of your father and mother, for they are owed by you. If you slaughter, you should plunder those you slaughter, for that is a sanctioned custom of the Prophet's".

Up to now, in response to these wars, we have observed two dominant approaches. One is the approach of what I call 'humanitarian peace'. This involves networks of international agencies, governments, NGOs and peacekeeping troops, who do their best to help civilians, provide humanitarian assistance, promote civil society and conflict resolution. The problem with this approach is that, despite good intentions, it does not help to control or eliminate fundamentalist networks. Through diplomatic talks, the warring parties are legitimised, and through humanitarian assistance, the wars are sustained. The other approach is casualty-free war – air strikes and economic sanctions against states linked into networks as in Yugoslavia in 1999, on-and-off against Iraq since 1991, or today against Afghanistan. While this approach has succeeded, with a bit of luck, in toppling hated regimes, it cannot contain the networks. On the contrary, evidence suggests that it may also stimulate networks. Politically, casualty-free war privileges western soldiers over civilians; it contributes to the formation of identity politics, of 'us' against 'them'. Economically, this approach further destroys the formal economy, leaving young men with little option other than to join the criminal networks as a way of making a living.

What we have learned about this kind of war is that the only possible exit route is political. There has to be a strategy of winning hearts and minds to counter the strategy of fear and hatred. There has to be an alternative politics based on tolerance and inclusiveness, which is capable of defeating the politics of intolerance and exclusion and capable of preserving the space for democratic politics. What is need is cosmopolitan, not western, politics; that is to say a politics which gives centrality to the individual and not to states and warring parties. To some extent, the humanitarian peace approach is based on the cosmopolitan assumption that all human beings are equal, but by eschewing the use of force this approach ends up privileging those with power. Casualty-free war is based on the assumption that states still control their territories and that Westerners are privileged.

An alternative cosmopolitan politics has to involve military action in order to protect civilians and create secure areas where cosmopolitan politics can develop. But it is military action that is more like law-enforcement than classic war; the aim is to protect civilians and catch war criminals, not to impose 'our will' on an enemy state. In these wars there is no such thing as military victory; the task of military action is to create conditions for an alternative politics. Devices like safe havens or humanitarian corridors, effectively defended, help protect and support civilians and establish an international presence on the ground. Tolerant politics cannot survive in conditions of violence – this is the point of the new wars. Military action may be needed to provide not national security but individual security. An alternative cosmopolitan politics also has to include an economic element, reconstruction and legitimate employment generating activities as an alternative to humanitarianism and the criminalised economy.

Where some progress has been made in the 'new wars', as in Northern Ireland and the Balkans (and it is always slow and tortuous since these wars are so much harder to end than to begin), what has made a difference has been the provision of security, including the capture of criminals, support for civil society and for democrats, and efforts at economic reconstruction.

In the case of the current new war, the dominant approach has been casualty-free war. Until 11 September, there was a tendency for Americans to assume that wars happen elsewhere. In effect, the United States acted as though it were the last nation-state, in which the priorities are domestic politics and what happens elsewhere doesn't matter. It was able to maintain the myth, so important to the American psyche, that there are still wars on the model of World War II, in which virtuous states triumph over evil states, and in which the United States can act as leader of the virtuous states at a distance. National missile defence is part of this myth; it would allow the United States to bomb evil states at a distance, safe in the knowledge that its territory is protected.

11 September exposed the vulnerability of the United States, and there was some hope that the US would act differently. This was a crime against humanity, not an attack on the United States. Perhaps Bush

would now abandon unilateralism. Tony Blair's speech to the Labour Party conference expressed the aspiration that this was a moment that could be seized for a new global politics.

However, in the initial reaction, the United Nations was sidelined. Far from being converted to multilateralism, the new global coalition of states was more reminiscent of the Cold War alliance. States that are ready to support the United States are part of the alliance, no matter what their domestic behaviour. Russia is in, despite its war crimes against Chechens; Pakistan, so recently an outcast because of its military coup and development of nuclear weapons, is a good guy again. And then there are Saudi Arabia, Israel and Uzbekistan, to name the most notorious. A state, Afghanistan, was identified as the enemy and a war from the air and by proxy has been conducted.

The toppling of the Taliban is, of course, an event to be welcomed. But the methods used may have the consequence of further polarisation between the West and Islam, even though Bush and others insist that this is a war against terrorism not Islam. The first strikes against Afghanistan did hand bin Laden a propaganda victory. His picture appeared beside Bush's on the backdrop to news broadcasts. Moreover, Bush's polarising language, demanding that everyone is either 'with us or with the terrorists' leaves no room for antiterrorist critics of the United States. We do live in a globalised world, and the frustrations in repressive societies cannot any longer be confined to particular territories. Those frustrations will not be expressed as democratic demands, as was the case in the Cold War period. They will be expressed in the language of extremes and in the acts of nihilism that characterise the new wars. The current approach might work for a few years by pouring money into repressive states and by killing known terrorists. But if the United States continues to act as a nation-state, wielding its military might to satisfy public demands for quick responses to acts of nihilism, the danger is that we will see a 'new war' on a global scale – a sort of global Israel/Palestine conflict with no equivalent to the international community to put pressure on the warring parties.

Just as the UN was sidelined, so was the humanitarian peace alternative: the humanitarian NGOs sat on the border in Pakistan warning of imminent catastrophe. The peace groups who protest against the bombing have been marginalised as apologists for terrorism just as, in the Cold War years, they were accused of being fellow travellers.

How would an alternative cosmopolitan approach be different? First, it would involve a serious effort to achieve global political legitimacy, to discredit the reasons why the West is seen as selective, partial, and insensitive. This would mean peace efforts in the Middle East, talks between Israel and Palestine, condemnation of all human rights violations in the area, and rethinking policy towards Iraq. It would also mean that this approach needs to be extended to other areas. The Balkans and Africa also need to be the recipients of cosmopolitan attention. If we pursue bin Laden and not Karadzic and Mladic, for example, we imply that we care more about American deaths than Bosnian deaths. Moreover, a cosmopolitan approach should not just be a governmental effort. The centrepiece of global legitimacy has to be a strong cosmopolitan constituency that can attract people of all cultures. What is important is to support and strengthen all civil society groups who press for multi-cultural values and work to bring different communities together in all parts of the world. People need to be mobilised not to fight but to defend cosmopolitan values.

Secondly, within Afghanistan there needs to be a commitment to the international rule of law, not war. Civilians must be protected and terrorists must be captured and brought before an international court. They must be treated as criminals and not military enemies. This means internationally sanctioned ground troops. Casualty-free war has succeeded in toppling the Taliban but at the cost of civilian deaths and the flight of Afghan refugees. Moreover, the al-Qaida network has not been destroyed. Most importantly perhaps, the unwillingness to risk casualties has left the hated Northern Alliance as the dominant presence on the ground, at least in the North, which makes the task of establishing a broad-based governments and creating security on the ground much more difficult. What is needed now is the presence of UN troops to protect humanitarian assistance and to establish security on the ground within an internationally sanctioned framework.

Finally, the economic environment of 'new wars' has to be taken into account – an environment that is conducive to criminal and fanatic activities. There has to be a new commitment to global justice; that is to say, serious concern about the victims of globalisation, the poor and the excluded, and, above all, about the criminalised informal transnational economy that is the underside of globalisation. This means not only the establishment of a rule of law and institution-building in the 'black holes', but also serious attention given to legitimate ways of making a living, a rethinking of international migration, and a rethinking of the policies of international financial institutions. In the end, the entrepreneurs of violence lead dangerous, risky lives, always on the edge of exhaustion and discovery. What they need is a more secure and stable alternative.

The opportunity for a cosmopolitan approach was lost immediately after 11 September, when the United States could command global sympathy. But it is still necessary to press for such an approach if not in order to avert a sustained global 'new war', then at least to mitigate its consequences.

Mary Kaldor is Principal Research Fellow and Programme Director at the Centre for the Study of Global Governance at the London School of Economics.

PART II

A Clash of Civilisations? – Identity and Hostility

4 Identity and Freedom

Amartya Sen

The dreadful events of 11 September have ushered in a period of terrible conflicts and war. Given the ongoing interest in what Samuel Huntington has called the 'clash of civilisations,' it is not surprising that many people have instantly seen a firm linkage between the conceptual divisions (especially on cultural or religious lines) and the manifest bloodshed that we see around us. There may well be a connection, but we have to ask what it is, and also whether the ideological vision of civilisational conflicts itself feeds some of the physical confrontations and violent engagements around the world.

At the root of much conflict lies a presumption – often implicitly held rather than explicitly articulated – that the people of the world can be uniquely categorised according to some singular and overarching system of partitioning. This singularly divisive view goes not only against the old-fashioned belief, which tends to be ridiculed these days (not entirely without reason) as much too soft-headed, that we human beings are all much the same, but also against the less discussed but much more plausible understanding that we are diversely different. Indeed, I would argue that the main hope of harmony in the contemporary world lies in the plurality of our identities, which cut across each other and work against sharp divisions around one single hardened line of impenetrable division. Our shared humanity gets savagely challenged when the confrontation is unified into one allegedly dominant system of classification; this is much more divisive than the universe of plural and diverse categorisations that shape the world in which we live. Plural diversity can be a great unifier in a way a unique system of intense divisions is not.

Plural divisions and singular confrontations

Indeed, we can be classified according to many competing systems of partitioning, each of which has far-reaching relevance in our lives:

nationalities, locations, classes, occupations, languages, politics, and many others. While religious categories have received much airing in recent years, they cannot be presumed to obliterate other distinctions, and even less taken to be the only relevant system of classifying people across the globe.[1] The recently championed civilisational classifications have often closely followed religious divisions. Samuel Huntington contrasts western civilisation with 'Islamic civilisation,' 'Hindu civilisation,' 'Buddhist civilisation,' etc., and while hybrid categories are accommodated (such as 'Sinic' or 'Japanese' civilisation), the alleged battlefronts of religious differences are incorporated into a carpentered vision of one dominant and hardened divisiveness.[2] By categorising all people into those belonging to 'the Islamic world,' 'the Christian world,' 'the Hindu world,' 'the Buddhist world,' etc., the divisive power of classificatory priority is implicitly used to place people firmly inside a unique set of rigid boxes. Other divisions (say, between the rich and the poor, between members of different classes and occupations, between people of different politics, between distinct nationalities and residential locations, between language groups, etc.) are all submerged by this allegedly pre-eminent way of seeing the differences between people.

The basic weakness of the thesis of 'clash of civilisation' lies in its programme of categorising people of the world according to the one – allegedly commanding – system of classification. The deficiency of the thesis thus begins well before we get to the point of asking whether civilisations must clash. No matter what answer we propose to give to this question, the form of the query itself pushes us into a narrow, arbitrary and deceptive way of thinking about the people of the world. And its power to befuddle can trap not only those who would like to support the thesis, but also those who would like to dispute it but respond within its prespecified terms of reference. To talk about 'the Islamic world' or 'the Hindu world' or 'the Christian world' is already to reduce people into this one dimension. Many opponents of the Huntington thesis (e.g. 'the West is not battling against the Islamic world') get, in effect, diverted into sharing the same narrow categorisation.

This vision of unique categorisation is both a serious epistemic mistake and is potentially a great ethical and political hazard. People do see themselves in very many different ways. A Bangladeshi Muslim is not only a Muslim but also a Bengali and a Bangladeshi, a Nepalese Hindu is not only a Hindu but also has political and ethnic characteristics that have their own relevance, and so on. Landless labourers struggling against exploitative landlords have things in common that cut across religious boundaries and even national ones. Poverty too can be a great source of solidarity across other boundaries. The kind of division highlighted by, say, the so-called 'anti-globalisation' protesters (which, incidentally, is one of the most globalised movements in the world) tries to unite the underdogs of the world economy, cutting right across religious or national or 'civilisational' lines of division. The multiplicity of categories works against rigid separation and its incendiary implications.

Civilisational innocence
In focusing on this one way of dividing the people of the world, the champions of the 'clash of civilisations' cut many corners. For example, in describing India as a 'Hindu civilisation,' Huntington's exposition of the alleged 'clash of civilisations' has to downplay the fact that India has more Muslims (about 125 million – more than the entire British and French populations put together) than any other country in the world with the exception of Indonesia and Pakistan. India may or may not be placed within the arbitrary definition of 'the Muslim world', but it is still the case that India has nearly as many Muslim citizens as does Pakistan (and a great many more than most countries in the so-called Muslim world). Also, it is impossible to think of 'the Indian civilisation' without taking note of the major role of Muslims in the history of India. Indeed, it is futile to try to have an understanding of the nature and range of Indian art, literature, music or food without seeing the extensive interactions across barriers of religious communities. India, Huntington has to note, is not just a Hindu civilisation.

Many Indians are proud of the fact that India is a secular country (unlike Pakistan which is an Islamic republic), and even though some political groups in India seem to be trying their best to overturn Indian secularism, nevertheless the secular constitution of India as well as the large majority in favour of secularism has, at least so far, kept these reactionary moves at bay. It is, however, important to acknowledge that it was a Muslim king – the Moghal emperor Akbar – who provided the most forceful and eloquent statement on the need for a secular state. It is true that the need for religious neutrality of the state had been enunciated nearly two millennia before Akbar by another Indian emperor, Ashoka, who had argued already in the third millennium BC for the tolerance and protection of different religions and had insisted that 'the sects of other people all deserve reverence for one reason or another'.[3] However, the continuity of public interest and legal scholarship connects Akbar's ideas and codifications with contemporary ideas and practice much more firmly than any other historical expression of Indian secularism.

Akbar's espousal of that approach not only involved actual practice, but also various legal pronouncements, such as: no one 'should be interfered with on account of religion, and anyone is to be allowed to go over to a religion that pleases him'.[4] (Given the delineating role that Huntington sees in the special history of the West as a champion of individual freedom and tolerance, it is perhaps worth mentioning that right at the time Akbar was making these pronouncements on religious tolerance, Giordano Bruno was burnt at the stake for heresy in Campo dei Fiori in Rome.) Akbar's overarching thesis took the form of arguing that the ultimate guiding rule has to be 'the pursuit of reason', rather than 'reliance on tradition'.[5] In line with his pursuit of what he called 'the path of reason' (rahi aql), Akbar insisted on the need for open dialogue and free choice, and also arranged recurrent discussions involving not only mainstream Muslim and Hindu philosophers, but also Christians, Jews, Parsees, Jains, and according to Abul Fazl (Akbar's intellectual ally), even the followers of 'Charvaka' – one of the Indian schools of atheistic thinking dating from around the sixth century BC.[6]

Aside from the relevance of all this in understanding the need to correct Huntington's view of India as a 'Hindu civilisation', these historical accounts raise the question as to whether Akbar had remained a real Muslim, despite his heterodox politics. This takes us back to the contemporary issue that is much discussed regarding the correct view of Islamic politics. Was Akbar being a good Muslim, or were his Muslim critics – of whom there were plenty in Delhi and Agra – the 'true' Muslims? That question demands a clear-cut answer if a Muslim is seen only in terms of his or her religion, without anything else being seen in the person. On the other hand if we take the view that being a Muslim is an important but not necessarily an overarching identity that determines everything else, then there is no need to resolve this political issue within the strict limits of religion. It is perhaps worth recollecting in this context that even though Akbar's political secularism and religious heterodoxy had supporters as well as detractors among influential Muslim groups, yet when he died in 1605 the Islamic theologian Abdul Haq, who had been very critical of Akbar for many of his beliefs and pronouncements, had to conclude that despite his 'innovations', Akbar had remained a good Muslim.[7] This is not puzzling at all if one's religion is not taken to be one's all-enveloping identity.

The basic issue, I would argue, is the need to recognise the plurality of our identities, and also the fact that, as responsible human beings, we have to choose ('through reason', as Akbar would argue), rather than inertly 'discover', what priorities to give to our diverse associations and affiliations. In contrast, the theorists of inescapable 'clashes' try, in effect, to deny strenuously, or to ignore implicitly, the relevance of multiple principles of classification, and related to that, the need for us all to take decisional responsibilities about our priorities.

Freedom and responsibility

Our religious or civilisational identity may well be very important, but it is one membership among many. The question we have to ask is not whether Islam (or Hinduism or Christianity) is a peace-loving religion or a combative one ('tell us which it is?'), but how a religious Muslim (or Hindu or Christian) may combine his or her religious beliefs or practices with other commitments and values, and other features of personal identity. To see the religious or in Huntington's sense 'civilisational' affiliation as an all-engulfing identity is itself a substantial mistake. There have been fierce warriors as well as great champions of peace among devoted members of each religion, and rather than asking which one is the true believer and which one a mere imposter, we should accept that one's religious faith does not in itself resolve all the decisions we have to take in our lives, including those concerning our political and social priorities and the corresponding issues of conduct and action. Both the proponents of peace and tolerance and the patrons of war and intolerance can belong to the same religion, and may be in their own ways true believers, without this being seen as a contradiction. The domain of one's religious identity does not vanquish all other aspects of one's understanding and affiliation.

While this is not the occasion to discuss it, this issue relates also to the public policy of placing children in denominational schools, where the knowledge of 'one's own culture' may sometimes come with a severe reduction of educational opportunities that could help inform choices on how to live. The purpose of education is not only to inform a child about different cultures in the world (including the one to which his or her family may, in one way or another, belong) but also to help the cultivation of reasoning and the exercise of freedom in later life. If identity was a monolithic characteristic, this would not have been as much of a worry as it clearly must be if the doors of choice are made much narrower for young Britons in the misguided belief that tradition makes choice unnecessary, thereby stifling what Akbar called 'the path of reason'.[8]

Concluding remarks

The principal problem with the perspective of 'clash of civilisations' does not lie in the unargued presumption that there must be such clashes (which is a subsequent issue – also deeply problematic but a later and derivative one). It lies rather in the partitioning of people of the world allegedly in a uniquely profound way – into distinct civilisations (whether or not they clash). This simplistic categorisation produces a misleading understanding of the people across the world and the diverse relations between them, and it also has the effect of magnifying a particular type of distinction to the exclusion of other important ones.

There are multiple features in our associations, affiliations and identities. We have to decide what importance, if any, to attach to each. Our religious beliefs or identities, whether chosen or simply inherited, cannot be asked to take over our entire life and all our reflective decisions. When a choice exists, to deny its existence is not only an epistemic failure, but also an ethical dereliction, since it allows a denial of responsibility that goes inescapably with the exercise of choice. The primary decisional issue that is being faced in the intellectual confrontations in the present conflicts does not arise from the esoteric debates on the 'true' nature of one religion or another (the newspapers have been full of quotations on different sides from the same scriptural document, such as the holy Koran), but from the importance of freedom and choice – and of personal responsibility that goes with choice – in what we decide to do (taking into account all our values and commitments, as well as our diverse affiliations and affinities).

There are many debates in Britain at this time on whether being a Muslim demands some kind of a strongly confrontational militancy, or whether (as the Prime Minister has put so eloquently) that it definitely does not. The Prime Minister's answer is certainly more than adequate as far as this question is concerned, but we must also ask whether the broader concerns should also be addressed through some further questions.

No one's religion can be his or her all-encompassing and exclusive identity. In particular Islam, as a religion, does not obliterate responsible choice for Muslims. Indeed, it is possible for one Muslim to take a confrontational view, and for another to be very tolerant of heterodoxy, without either of them ceasing to be a Muslim for that reason. This is not only because the idea of 'ijtehad' or religious interpretation allows considerable latitude, but also because there are differences of views as to how much latitude ijtehad does allow.

To focus solely on the grand religious classification is not only to miss other significant concerns and ideas that move people; it also has the effect of lessening the importance of other priorities by artificially magnifying the voice of religious authority. The mullahs are then treated as the ex officio spokesmen for the so-called 'Islamic world', even though a great many Muslims have profound differences with what is proposed by one Mullah or another. The same would apply to Christian or Hindu religious leaders' being seen as the spokespeople for their 'flocks'. The singular classification not only makes provisional distinctions into rigidly inflexible barriers, but also gives a commanding voice to the 'establishment' figures in those categories, while others are silenced and muffled.

The robust source of unity in the world is not just what we have in common as human beings (even though that is not an inconsiderable list), but also the multiplicity of our diversities. We may not be quite the same, but we are different from each other in very many different ways. Our religious or 'civilisational' identification may be important, but not uniquely so. The supreme cliche of the contemporary world takes the form of asking, 'Do civilisations clash?' We have at least as good a reason to be sceptical of that question as we have to try to answer it. Indeed, no matter how we answer that question, we end up endorsing, if only implicitly, that the people of the world can be sensibly seen in terms of a singular partitioning between 'civilisations'. The world is richer than that.

Amartya Sen is Master of Trinity College, University of Cambridge.

[1] I have discussed this and related issues in my 1998 Romanes Lecture at Oxford, published *as: Reason before Identity* (Oxford: Oxford University Press, 1999).

[2] Samuel P. Huntington, *The Clash of Civilizations and the Remaking of the World Order* (New York: Simon & Schuster, 1996).

[3] Translation in Vincent A. Smith, *Asoka* (Delhi: S. Chand, 1964), pp. 170-1.

[4] Translation in Vincent Smith, *Akbar: the Great Mogul* (Oxford: Clarendon Press, 1917), p. 257.

[5] See Irfan Habib, ed., *Akbar and His India* (Delhi and New York: Oxford University Press, 1997) for a set of fine essays investigating the beliefs and policies of Akbar as well as the intellectual influences that led him to his heterodox position.

[6] Habib, ed., *Akbar and His India* (1997), pp. 97-8.

[7] See Iqtidar Alam Khan, Akbar's Personality Traits and World Outlook: A Critical Reappraisal, in Habib, *Akbar and His India*, p. 78.

[8] I have tried to discuss this issue in my Annual Lecture to the British Academy for 2000, *Other People*, to be published by the British Academy (shorter version published in *The New Republic*, December 2000).

5 Why Muslims hate the West and what we can do about it

Fareed Zakaria

There are billions of poor and weak and oppressed people around the world. They don't turn planes into bombs. They don't blow themselves up to kill thousands of civilians. If envy were the cause of terrorism, Beverly Hills, Fifth Avenue and Mayfair would have become morgues long ago. We've heard a lot of discussion in recent weeks about the causative link between poverty and terrorism. There's an appealing simplicity to the argument, coupled with a sense of broad-minded historical wisdom. But there is something stronger at work here than deprivation and jealousy. That bin Laden has not found universal condemnation in the Islamic world is certainly ample evidence that, whatever the oddity he is, he should not be seen as some kind of historical aberration, a curiosity to be siphoned off from the main narrative of world history – like Timothy McVeigh or the Unabomber. Bin Laden is an extreme expression of a deep-seated systemic malaise within the Arab world.

In some ways the Arab world seems less ready to confront the age of globalisation even than Africa, despite the devastation that continent has suffered from AIDS and economic and political dysfunction. At least the Africans want to adapt to the new global economy. The Arab world has not yet taken that first step. Modernisation is now taken to mean, inevitably, uncontrollably, westernisation and, even worse, Americanisation. This fear has paralysed Arab civilisation, making economic advance impossible and political progress fraught with difficulty.

The West thinks of modernity as all good – and it has been almost all good for them. But for the Arab world, modernity has been one failure after another. Each path followed – socialism, secularism, nationalism

– has turned into a dead end. 30 or 40 years ago it was not unusual for countries to be ruled by dictators implementing dirigiste policies. But over the decades while other countries adjusted to their failures, Arab regimes got stuck in their ways. As a result in a startling inversion of recent patterns, most Arab countries today are less free than they were 30 years ago.

Those few that reformed economically could not bring themselves to ease up politically. The Shah of Iran, the Middle Eastern ruler who tried to move his country into the modern era fastest, reaped the most violent reaction in the Iranian revolution of 1979. But even the Shah's modernisation – compared, for example, with the East Asian approach of hard work, investment and thrift – was an attempt to buy modernisation with oil wealth. It turns out that modernisation takes more than strongmen and oil money. Importing foreign stuff – Cadillacs, Gulfstreams and McDonald's – is easy. Importing the inner stuffing of modern society – a free market, political parties, accountability and the rule of law – is difficult and dangerous. The gulf states, for example, have had modernisation-lite, with the goods and even the workers imported from abroad. Nothing was homegrown; nothing is even now. As for politics, the gulf governments offered their people a bargain: we will bribe you with wealth, but in return let us stay in power. It was the inverse slogan of the American revolution – no taxation, but no representation either.

The new age of globalisation has hit the Arab world in a very strange way. Its societies are open enough to be disrupted by modernity, but not so open that they can ride the wave. They see the television shows, the fast foods and the fizzy drinks. But they don't see genuine liberalisation in the society, with increased opportunities and greater openness. Globalisation in the Arab world is the critic's caricature of globalisation – a slew of Western products and billboards with little else. For some in their societies it means more things to buy. For the regimes it is an unsettling, dangerous phenomenon. As a result, the people they rule can look at globalisation but for the most part not touch it.

Disoriented young men, with one foot in the old world and another in the new, now look for a purer, simpler alternative. Fundamentalism searches for such people everywhere; it, too, has been globalised – with the help of vast funds from Saudi Arabia. One can now find men in Indonesia who regard the Palestinian cause as their own. (Twenty years ago an Indonesian Muslim would barely have known where Palestine was.) Often these young men learned to reject the West while they were in the West. As did Mohamed Atta, the Hamburg-educated engineer who drove the first plane into the World Trade Center.

The Arab world has a problem with its Attas in more than one sense. Globalisation has caught it at a bad demographic moment. Arab societies are going through a massive youth bulge, with more than half of most countries' populations under the age of 25. Young men, often better educated than their parents, leave their traditional villages to find work. They arrive in noisy, crowded cities like Cairo, Beirut and Damascus or go to work in the oil states. (Almost 10 per cent of Egypt's working population worked in the gulf at one point.) In their new world they see great disparities of wealth and the disorienting effects of modernity; most unsettlingly, they see women, unveiled and in public places, taking buses, eating in cafes and working alongside them.

A huge influx of restless young men in any country is bad news. When accompanied by even small economic and social change, it usually produces a new politics of protest. In the past, societies in these circumstances have fallen prey to a search for revolutionary solutions. (France went through a youth bulge just before the French Revolution, as did Iran before its 1979 revolution.) In the case of the Arab world, this revolution has taken the form of an Islamic resurgence.

Why religion?

As the regimes of the Middle East grew more distant and oppressive and hollow in the decades following Nasser, fundamentalism's appeal grew. It flourished because the Muslim Brotherhood and organisations like it at least tried to give people a sense of meaning and purpose in a changing world, something no leader in the Middle East tried to do.

On that score, Islam had little competition. The Arab world is a political desert with no real political parties, no free press, few pathways for dissent. As a result, the mosque turned into the place to discuss politics. And fundamentalist organisations have done more than talk. From the Muslim Brotherhood to Hamas to Hezbollah, they actively provide social services, medical assistance, counselling and temporary housing. For those who treasure civil society, it is disturbing to see that in the Middle East these illiberal groups are civil society. Sheri Berman, a scholar at Princeton who studies the rise of fascist parties in Europe, explains a striking historical parallel. 'Fascists were often very effective at providing social services,' she pointed out. 'When the state or political parties fail to provide a sense of legitimacy or purpose or basic services, other organisations have often been able to step into the void. In Islamic countries there is a ready-made source of legitimacy in the religion.'

Intellectuals, disillusioned by the half-baked or over-rapid modernisation that was throwing their world into turmoil, were writing books against 'Westoxification' and calling the modern Iranian man – half western, half eastern – rootless. Fashionable intellectuals, often writing from the comfort of London or Paris, would critique American secularism and consumerism and endorse an Islamic alternative. As theories like these spread across the Arab world, they appealed not to the poorest of the poor, for whom westernisation was magical (it meant food and medicine). They appealed to the half-educated hordes entering the cities of the Middle East or seeking education and jobs in the West.

The biggest Devil's bargain has been made by the moderate monarchies of the Persian Gulf, particularly Saudi Arabia. The Saudi regime has played a dangerous game. It deflects attention from its shoddy record at home by funding religious schools (madrasas) and centres that sprcad a rigid, puritanical brand of Islam – Wahhabism. In the past 30 years Saudi-funded schools have churned out tens of thousands of half-educated, fanatical Muslims who view the modern world and non-Muslims with great suspicion. America in this world view is almost always evil.

This exported fundamentalism has in turn infected not just other Arab societies but countries outside the Arab world, like Pakistan. During the 11-year reign of General Zia ul-Haq, the dictator decided that as he squashed political dissent he needed allies. He found them in the fundamentalists. With the aid of Saudi financiers and functionaries, he set up scores of madrasas throughout the country. They bought him temporary legitimacy but have eroded the social fabric of Pakistan.

If there is one great cause of the rise of Islamic fundamentalism, it is the total failure of political institutions in the Arab world. Muslim elites have averted their eyes from this reality. Conferences at Islamic centres would still rather discuss 'Islam and the Environment' than examine the dysfunctions of the current regimes. But as the moderate majority looks the other way, Islam is being taken over by a small, poisonous element, people who advocate cruel attitudes toward women, education, the economy and modern life in general.

International history

If almost any Arab were to have read this essay so far, he would have objected vigorously by now. 'It is all very well to talk about the failures of the Arab world,' he would say, 'but what about the failures of the West? You speak of long-term decline, but our problems are with specific, cruel American policies.' For most Arabs, relations with the United States have been filled with disappointment.

While the Arab world has long felt betrayed by Europe's colonial powers, its disillusionment with America begins most importantly with the creation of Israel in 1948. As the Arabs see it, at a time when colonies were winning independence from the West, here was a state largely composed of foreign people being imposed on a region with western backing. The anger deepened in the wake of America's support for Israel during the wars of 1967 and 1973, and ever since in its relations with the Palestinians. The daily exposure to Israel's iron-fisted rule over the occupied territories has turned this into the great cause of the Arab – and indeed the broader Islamic – world. Elsewhere, they look at American policy in the region as cynically geared to America's oil interests, supporting thugs and tyrants without any hesitation. Finally, the bombing and isolation of Iraq have become fodder for daily attacks on the United States. While many in the Arab world do not like Saddam Hussein, they believe that the United States has chosen a particularly inhuman method of fighting him – a method that is starving an entire nation.

There is substance to some of these charges, and certainly from the point of view of an Arab, American actions are never going to seem entirely fair. Like any country, America has its interests. In my view, America's greatest sins toward the Arab world are sins of omission. We have neglected to press any regime there to open up its society. This neglect turned deadly in the case of Afghanistan. Walking away from that fractured country after 1989 resulted in the rise of bin Laden and the Taliban. America has not been venal in the Arab world. But it has been careless.

Yet carelessness is not enough to explain Arab rage. After all, if concern for the Palestinians is at the heart of the problem, why have their Arab brethren done nothing for them? (They cannot resettle in any Arab nation but Jordan, and the aid they receive from the gulf states is minuscule.) Israel treats its one million Arabs as second-class citizens, a disgrace to its democracy. And yet the tragedy of the Arab world is that Israel accords them more political rights and dignities than most Arab nations give to their own people. Why is the focus of Arab anger on Israel and not those regimes?

The disproportionate feelings of grievance directed at America have to be placed in the overall context of the sense of humiliation, decline and despair that sweeps the Arab world. After all, the Chinese vigorously disagree with most of America's foreign policy and have fought wars with US proxies. African states feel the same sense of disappointment and unfairness. But they do not work it into a violent rage against America. Arabs, however, feel that they are under siege from the modern world and that the United States symbolises this world. Thus every action America takes gets magnified a thousandfold. And even when we do not act, the rumours of our gigantic powers and nefarious deeds still spread. Most Americans would not believe how common the rumour is throughout the Arab world that either the CIA or Israel's Mossad blew up the World Trade Center to justify attacks on Arabs and Muslims. This is the culture from which the suicide bombers have come.

The way forward: the new New World Order

We must now devise a strategy for the post-Cold War era, one that addresses America's principal national security need and yet is sustained by a broad international consensus. To do this we will have to give up some Cold War reflexes, such as an allergy to multilateralism, and stop insisting that China is about to rival us militarily or that Russia is likely to re-emerge as a new military threat. (For ten years now, our defence forces have been aligned for everything but the real danger we face. This will inevitably change.)

The purpose of an international coalition is practical and strategic. Given the nature of this 'war on terrorism', we will need the constant co-operation of other governments – to make arrests, shut down safe houses, close bank accounts and share intelligence. Alliance politics has become a matter of high national security. But there is a broader imperative. The United States dominates the world in a way that inevitably arouses envy or anger or opposition. That comes with the power, but we still need to get things done. If we can mask our power in – sorry, work with – institutions like the United Nations Security Council, US might will be easier for much of the world to bear. George Bush senior understood this, which is why he ensured that the United Nations sanctioned the Gulf War. The point here is to succeed, and international legitimacy can help us do that.

However, we should not pursue mistaken policies simply out of spite. Our policy towards Saddam is broken. We have no inspectors in Iraq, the sanctions are – for whatever reason – starving Iraqis and he continues to build chemical and biological weapons. There is a way to reorient our policy to focus our pressure on Saddam and not his people, contain him militarily but not harm common Iraqis economically. Colin Powell has been trying to do this; he should be given leeway to try again. In time we will have to address the broader question of what to do about Saddam, a question that, unfortunately, does not have an easy answer. On Israel we should make a clear distinction between its right to exist and its occupation of the West Bank and Gaza. On the first we should be as unyielding as ever; on the second we should continue trying to construct a final deal along the lines that Bill Clinton and Ehud Barak outlined. I suggest that we do this less because it will lower the temperature in the Arab world – who knows if it will? – than because it's the right thing to do. Israel cannot remain a democracy and continue to occupy and militarily rule three million people against their wishes. It's bad for Israel, bad for the Palestinians and bad for the international community.

But policy changes, large or small, are not at the heart of the struggle we face. The third, vital component to this battle is a cultural strategy. The United States must help Islam enter the modern world. It sounds like an impossible challenge, and it certainly is not one we would have chosen. But America – indeed the whole world – faces a dire security threat that will not be resolved unless we can stop the political, economic and cultural collapse that lies at the roots of Arab rage. During the Cold War the West employed myriad ideological strategies to discredit the appeal of communism, make democracy seem attractive and promote open societies. We will have to do something on that scale to win this cultural struggle.

First, we have to help 'moderate' Arab states, but on the condition that they really do embrace moderation. For too long regimes like Saudi Arabia's have engaged in a deadly dance with religious extremism. Even Egypt, which has always denounced fundamentalism, allows its controlled media to rant crazily about America and Israel. (That way they don't rant about the dictatorship they live under.) But more broadly, we must persuade Arab moderates to make the case to their people that Islam is compatible with modern society, that it does allow women to work, that it encourages education and that it has welcomed people of other faiths and creeds. Some of this they will do – 11 September has been a wake-up call for many. The Saudi regime denounced and broke its ties to the Taliban (a regime that it used to glorify as representing pure Islam). The United States and the West should do their own work as well. We can fund moderate Muslim groups and scholars and broadcast fresh thinking across the Arab world, all aimed at breaking the power of the fundamentalists.

Obviously we have to help construct a new political order in Afghanistan as the last vestiges of the Taliban regime are removed. But beyond that we have to press the nations of the Arab world – and others, like Pakistan, where the virus of fundamentalism has spread – to reform, open up and gain legitimacy. We need to do business with these regimes; yet, just as we did with South Korea and Taiwan during the Cold War, we can ally with these dictatorships and still push them towards reform. For those who argue that we should not engage in nation-building, I would say foreign policy is not theology. I have myself been sceptical of nation-building in places where our interests were unclear and it seemed unlikely that we would stay the course. In this case, stable political development is the key to reducing our single greatest security threat. We have no option but to get back into the nation-building business. If the West can help Islam enter modernity in dignity and peace, it will have done more than achieved security. It will have changed the world.

Fareed Zakaria is Editor of *Newsweek*.

6 A Civilisational Challenge

Kanan Makiya

In the wake of 11 September, the Arab and Muslim worlds confront a civilisational challenge unlike any they have faced since the fall of the Ottoman Empire. For, in years to come, the greatest price to be paid for the apocalyptic acts unleashed on New York and Washington may be borne not by the victims of the terrorists, but by all individual Arabs or Muslims wherever they live. This price does not include the bombing in Afghanistan or efforts to hunt down Muslim and Arab terrorists from the suburbs of Boston to the student hostels of Hamburg to the alleyways of Cairo, or the daily humiliations such hunts may impose. The greatest long-term damage will done if Muslims and Arabs respond to 11 September by wallowing even more in their sense of victimhood.

'Anti-Americanism' in the hands of Osama bin Laden after 11 September is but the latest and most virulent variant of an idea nurtured originally by secular, so-called progressive, nationalist Arab intellectuals under a variety of different earlier labels: anti-imperialism, anti-zionism, Arab socialism, pan-Arabism. These took as their point of departure genuine grievances, some more legitimate than others.

Among the legitimate grievances, priority of place must be given to the profound injustice caused by the real dispossession of millions of Palestinians that accompanied the birth and consolidation of the state of Israel in 1948. In the hands of Arab nationalists and leftist 'anti-imperialists' of my generation (of whom I was one), however, this sense of grievance failed to get channelled into building civil societies based on any hard-won expansions of civil liberties wrested from tyrannical regimes (such as happened in Latin America in the 1980s). Our failure even to pursue such goals, from the 1960s through to the 1980s, left a vacuum which was soon filled by a conspiratorial view of history, reinforced by those consolidating tyrannical regimes, which ascribed all of the ills of one's own world to either the great Satan, America, or the little Satan, Israel.

The dangerous, unstated corollary of this view was the notion that 'we Arabs' had no, or hardly any, agency to change the terribly unjust way that the world works. Arabs in particular, and Muslims more generally, increasingly began to see themselves as the great victims of the second half of the 20th century, consigned to a Sisyphean struggle against absolute or Satanic injustice. Lost was a sense of ourselves as authentic political agents aiming toward concrete and gradual gains in the political arena.

It is important to note that Arabs are not the only ones to wrap themselves up in the comforting mantle of victimhood; the modern Israeli sense of identity was, after all, forged on the foundations of the Holocaust just as surely as Palestinian national identity was forged by Israel's harsh treatment of Palestinians. Such symmetries (and there are many others) have created a powerful complex of victimhood which undermines all reconciliation efforts (like Oslo), and which is applicable to one degree or another to all peoples of the Middle East (Palestinians, Israelis, Kurds, Armenians, Chaldean Christians, Turkomans, Shi'is, and Sunnis).

In the Arab world, especially after Israel's victory in the Six Day War of 1967, this complex turned itself into the driving force of politics and culture; it became the foundation upon which such murderous regimes as Saddam Hussein's Iraq and Hafez Assad's Syria were built. From the hands of secular Arab nationalists, the murderous anti-American brew was passed on to (previously marginal) religious zealots. In 1979 it fused with anti-Shah sentiments to become one of the animating forces of the Iranian revolution. In the wake of that seminal event, it overwhelmed major sections of the Islamic movement from Algeria to Pakistan.

A 'politics of victimhood' is inherently unreasonable. In the Arab part of the Middle East that inherent unreasonableness (as typical of Israelis as of Kurds, for instance) is fuelled by failure. The Arab world today comprises a veritable cauldron of collapsing economies and mass unemployment overseen by ever more repressive regimes. This is a world that has been defeated repeatedly in one war after another with Israel. Civil war in tiny Lebanon alone killed 140,000 people, wounded 400,000, and made refugees of one in every three Lebanese. The eight-year Iran-Iraq war killed more people than all the Arab-Israeli wars rolled into one. But in many ways the greatest failure of all has been intellectual, specifically a failure of the intelligentsia – writers, professors, artists, journalists, and so forth – who, with few exceptions, failed to challenge their respective regimes' wildest and most paranoid fantasies. If anything, they buttressed them by refusing to break out of nationalist paradigms (for instance by not extending the hand of solidarity to their counterparts in Israel).

Instead they acted as 'rejectionist' critics who largely excoriate their own regimes for being insufficiently anti-zionist or anti-imperialist. Lost in all of this is the hard work of creating a modern, rights-based political order from those very regimes, one which could eventually form the basis for a wider-based, general prosperity. In the absence of that kind of alternative focus, in the thick of all that endlessly self-pitying victimising rhetoric, is it any wonder that despairing middle-class individuals gravitate towards ever more radical and terrorist activities aimed at smiting the demonised Other? And that their horrific suicidal actions in turn call forth ever more summary and violent responses, which in turn further reinforce that pervasive sense of victimhood, yielding up further delusional martyrs?

In the five-page letter written by one of the hijackers and left in a suitcase in the car park of Boston's airport, a passage giving guidance to the hijackers in case they meet resistance from one of the American passengers appears:

'If God grants any one of you a slaughter, you should perform it as an offering on behalf of your father and mother, for they are owed by you. Do not disagree among yourselves, but listen and obey. If you slaughter, you should plunder those you slaughter, for that is a sanctioned custom of the Prophet's, on the condition that you do not get occupied with the plunder so that you would leave what is more important, such as paying attention to the enemy, his treachery and attacks. That is because such action is very harmful [to the mission].'

Such a reading of the Koran to justify the mass killing of civilians is as Islamic as a reading of the story of Sodom and Gommorah to justify nuclear holocaust on the new Babylon that is New York. This is not Islam any more than the Ku Klux Klan is Christianity. No concessions can or should be made to such mindsets, which have more in common with one another than they do with the religions they claim to represent.

To argue, as many Arabs and Muslims are doing today (and not a few liberal and left-leaning western voices), that 'Americans should ask themselves why they are so hated in the world,' is to make such a concession; it is to provide a justification, however unwittingly, for this kind of warped mindset. The thinking is the same as the 'linkage' dreamed up by Saddam Hussein when he tried to get the Arab world to believe that he had occupied Kuwait in 1990 in order to liberate Palestine. Large numbers of intellectuals allowed themselves to think back then, that perhaps Iraq's much touted military strength would act as a counterweight to Israeli arrogance, forcing Israel to make concessions it would not otherwise make. There were those who argued that Kuwait was hardly worth fighting for, being an artificial creation of the oil companies. More technocratic types convinced themselves that Saddam could be prevailed upon by the Arab League to leave of his own accord. They tended to think that negotiations over Iraqi withdrawal before the outbreak of hostilities only broke down because of American perfidy and desire to pursue a war strategy at all costs.

The difference between this kind of reasoning during the 1990-91 Gulf crisis and today is that if the argument was intellectually vacuous then, it is a thousand times more so now. Bin Laden is a far more unconvincing convert to the Palestinian cause than Saddam Hussein was in 1990-91. The cardinal sin of America, according to Bin Laden, is one of polluting 'the land of Muhammad', the phrase he used in his 2001 al-Jazeera video clip. Worse than being wrong, however, applying the reasoning that was used in 1990-1991 is morally bankrupt, to say nothing of being totally counterproductive. For every attempt to 'rationalise' or 'explain' the new anti-Americanism rampant in so much of the Muslim and Arab worlds bolsters the project of the perpetrators of the heinous act of 11 September, which is to blur the lines that separate their sect of a few hundred people from the hundreds of millions of ordinary peace-loving Muslims and Arabs in the world.

Mercifully, the very same Western leaders that are engaged in the 'war against terrorism' are trying hard, and genuinely, to say that their efforts are not directed at Muslims and Arab or Muslim culture. Constantly they are being seen with Muslim clerics and visiting mosques. That is all for the good. But it is not enough to turn the tide of public opinion which will increasingly need and want to know who is the 'other' in this coming war.

Terrorism is a tactic, after all, not a side. And the terrorist 'grand alliance' that bin Laden began to assemble in the 1990s is not only targeted at the West; its ultimate target is the whole post-Ottoman Arab order. This is a revolt of the sons against the fathers who had to make all the compromises and broker all the dirty little deals that created the constellation of ultimately failed states that we see today in the Middle East. The great uncle of bin Laden's right-hand man, Ayman al-Zawahiri, for instance, was the first secretary general of the Arab League set up in the wake of the fall of the Ottoman Empire, while Osama himself is a son of the mega-rich generation which, literally in the case of bin Laden's father, built modern Saudi Arabia. Such would-be leaders are a far cry from thugs like Saddam Hussein, Muammar al-Gadhafi, and Hafez al-Asad, all of whom rose to power from lowly beginnings in nondescript towns and villages through political parties or state institutions like the army and the secret police.

Use of the word 'war' in these complex circumstances of what is at bottom a war of Arab against Arab, however understandable, was a strategic mistake by the American president in the battle for hearts and minds in the Arab Middle East. For, like the war on drugs or the war on poverty, it inculcates expectations at the risk of showing few or very inconclusive results. The problem is much deeper than bin Laden and his associates, and will not end with their demise. Nor is it about Islam and its relation with the West; it is above all about the mess that the Arab part of the Muslim world is in, and that part is some seventeen per cent of the whole. As I wrote in *Cruelty and Silence*, quoting the 1930s Iraqi *alter ego* of Tom Lehrer, Aziz Ali, *Da' illi beena, minna wa feena*, 'the disease that is in us, is from us and within us.' Against this kind of enemy the West can do nothing. We have to do it ourselves.

Bin Laden's apocalypse, like that of the Russian nihilists of the nineteenth century, is not going to materialise. He will be defeated. The outcome of this first phase of President Bush's 'war against terrorism' is no longer in doubt. The important question is: what will its demise mean for a world whose own failures are responsible for creating the bin Laden monster in the first place? So many threads of what happened on 11 September lead back to the 1991 Gulf War, to how that war was waged, and above all to the irresponsible way in which it was left unfinished. The Palestinian question, foundational though it is for the peace of the whole region, is just one, and by no means even the most important, of those threads. There is no easy explanation, no one wrong, or great act of historical injustice, that lies behind what happened on 11 September.

In the final analysis Muslims and Arabs, not Americans, have to be on the frontlines of a new kind of war, one that is worth waging for their own salvation and in their own souls. And that, as good out-of-fashion Muslim scholars will tell you, is the true meaning of 'jihad', a meaning that has been hijacked by terrorists and suicide bombers and all those who applaud or find excuses for them. To exorcise what they have done in our name is the civilisational challenge that Arabs and Muslims within and without the Arab and Muslim worlds (Osama bin Laden has erased the significance of such distinctions) face at the dawn of the 21st century.

Kanan Makiya was born in Baghdad, Iraq and now teaches at Brandeis University. His books include *Republic of Fear: The Politics of Modern Iraq* (University of California Press, 1989 and 1995), *Cruelty and Silence: War, Tyranny, Uprising and the Arab World* (Penguin, 1993) and the newly published *The Rock: A Seventh Century Tale of Jerusalem* (Pantheon Books, 2001).

PART III

Globalisation – Changing Relationships and Changing Responsibilities

7   Violence, Law and Justice
in a Global Age

David Held

'It's the worst thing that's happened, but only this week. Two years ago, an earthquake in Turkey killed 17,000 people in a day, babies and mothers and businessmen…. The November before that, a hurricane hit Honduras and Nicaragua and killed even more…. Which end of the world shall we talk about? Sixty years ago, Japanese airplanes bombed Navy boys who were sleeping on ships in gentle Pacific waters. Three and a half years later, American planes bombed a plaza in Japan where men and women were going to work, where schoolchildren were playing, and more humans died at once than anyone thought possible. Seventy thousand in a minute. Imagine….

There are no worst days, it seems. Ten years ago, early on a January morning, bombs rained down from the sky and caused great buildings in the city of Baghdad to fall down – hotels, hospitals, palaces, buildings with mothers and soldiers inside – and here in the place I want to love best, I had to watch people cheering about it. In Baghdad, survivors shook their fists at the sky and said the word "evil". When many lives are lost all at once, people gather together and say words like "heinous" and "honor" and "revenge"…. They raise up their compatriots' lives to a sacred place – we do this, all of us who are human – thinking our own citizens to be more worthy of grief and less willingly risked than lives on other soil.' (Barbara Kingsolver, *Los Angeles Times*, 23 September 2001)

This is an unsettling and challenging passage. When I first read it, I felt angered and unsympathetic to its call to think systematically about the

11 September in the context of other disasters, acts of aggression and wars. A few days later I found it helpful to connect its sentiments to my own strong cosmopolitan orientations.

Immanuel Kant wrote over two hundred years ago that we are 'unavoidably side by side'. A violent challenge to law and justice in one place has consequences for many other places and can be experienced everywhere. While he dwelt on these matters and their implications at length, he could not have known how profound and immediate his concerns would become.

Since Kant, our mutual interconnectedness and vulnerability have grown rapidly. We no longer live, if we ever did, in a world of discrete national communities. Instead, we live in a world of what I like to call 'overlapping communities of fate' where the trajectories of countries are heavily enmeshed with each other. In our world, it is not only the violent exception that links people together across borders; the very nature of everyday problems and processes joins people in multiple ways.

The story of our increasingly global order – 'globalisation' – is not a singular one. There has been an expansion of global markets which has altered the political terrain, increasing exit options for capital of all kinds, and putting pressure on polities everywhere.[1] But the story of globalisation is not just economic; it is also one of growing aspirations for international law and justice. From the UN system to the EU, from changes to the laws of war to the entrenchment of human rights, from the emergence of international environmental regimes to the foundation of the International Criminal Court, there is also another narrative being told – a narrative which seeks to reframe human activity and entrench it in law, rights and responsibilities. In the first section of this essay, I would like to reflect on this second narrative and highlight some of its strengths and limitations. Once this background is sketched, elements of the legal and political context of the 11 September can be better grasped, particularly the growing tension between the aims of economic globalisation on the one hand, and the search for international justice on the other.

Reframing human activity: International law, rights and responsibilities

The process of the gradual delimitation of political power, and the increasing significance of international law and justice, can be illustrated by reflecting on a strand in international legal thinking which has overturned the exclusive position of the state in international law, and buttressed the role of the individual in relation to, and with responsibility for, systematic violence against others.

In the first instance, by recognising the legal status of conscientious objection, many states – particularly western states (I shall return to the significance of this later) – have acknowledged there are clear occasions when an individual has a moral obligation beyond that of his or her obligation as a citizen of a state.[2] The refusal to serve in a national army triggers a claim to a 'higher moral court' of rights and duties. Such claims are exemplified as well in the changing legal position of those who are willing go to war. The recognition in international law of the offences of war crimes, genocide and crimes against humanity makes clear that acquiescence to the commands of national leaders will not be considered sufficient grounds for absolving individual guilt in these cases. A turning-point in this regard was the judgement of the International Tribunal at Nuremberg (and the parallel tribunal in Tokyo). The tribunal laid down, for the first time in history, that when international rules that protect basic humanitarian values are in conflict with state laws, every individual must transgress the state laws (except where there is no room for 'moral choice', i.e. when a gun is being held to someone's head).[3] Modern international law has generally endorsed the position taken by the tribunal, and has affirmed its rejection of the defence of obedience to superior orders in matters of responsibility for crimes against peace and humanity.

The most notable recent extension of the application of the Nuremberg principles has been the establishment of the war crimes tribunals for the former Yugoslavia (established by the UN Security Council in 1993) and for Rwanda (set up in 1994). The Yugoslav tribunal has issued indictments against people from all three ethnic groups in Bosnia, and is investigating crimes in Kosovo, although it has encountered serious difficulty in obtaining custody of some of the key accused. (Significantly, of course, ex-President Slobodan Milosevic has been arrested and brought before The Hague war crimes tribunal – his trial continues.) Although neither the tribunal for Rwanda nor the Yugoslav tribunal have had the ability to detain and try more than a small fraction of those engaged in atrocities, both have taken important steps toward implementing the law governing war crimes and thereby reducing the credibility gap between the promises of such law, on the one hand, and the weakness of its application, on the other.

Most recently, the proposals put forward for the establishment of a permanent International Criminal Court (ICC) are designed to help close this gap in the longer term.[4] Several major obstacles remain to its successful creation, including the continuing opposition from the United States (which fears its soldiers will be the target of politically-motivated prosecutions) and dependency upon individual state consent for its effectiveness.[5] However, it is likely that the Court will be formally established (with or without the USA) and will mark another significant step away from the classic regime of state sovereignty – sovereignty, that is, as effective power – towards the firm establishment of the 'liberal regime of international sovereignty' as I refer to it – sovereignty shaped and delimited by new broader frameworks of governance and law.[6]

The ground now being staked out in international legal agreements suggests something of particular importance: that the containment of armed aggression and abuses of power can only be achieved both through the control of warfare and the prevention of the abuse of human rights. For it is only too apparent that many forms of violence perpetrated against individuals, and many forms of abuse of power, do not take place during declared acts of war. In fact it can be argued that the distinctions between war and peace as well as between aggression and repression, are eroded by changing patterns of violence. The kinds of violence witnessed in Bosnia and Kosovo highlight the role of paramilitaries and of organised crime, and the use of parts of national armies which may no longer be under the direct control of a state. What these kinds of violence signal is that there is a very fine line between explicit formal crimes committed during acts of national war, and major attacks on the welfare and physical integrity of citizens in situations that may not involve a declaration of war by states. While many of the new forms of warfare do not fall directly under the classic rules of war, they are massive violations of international human rights. Accordingly, the rules of war and human rights law can be seen as two complementary forms of international rules which aim to circumscribe the proper form, scope and use of coercive power. For all the limitations on their enforcement, these are significant changes which, when taken together, amount to the rejection of the doctrine of legitimate power as effective control, and its replacement by international rules which establish basic humanitarian values as the criteria for legitimate government.

How do the terrorist attacks on the World Trade Center and the Pentagon fit into this pattern of legal change? A wide variety of legal instruments, dating back to 1963 (the Convention on Offences and Certain Other Acts Committed on Board Aircraft), enable the international community to take action against terrorism, and bring those responsible to justice. If the persons responsible for the 11 September attacks can be identified and apprehended, they could face prosecution in virtually any country that obtains custody of them. In particular the widely ratified Hague Convention for the Suppression of Unlawful Seizure of Aircraft (1970) makes the highjacking of aircraft an international criminal offence. The offence is regarded as extraditable under any extradition treaty in force between contracting states, and applies to accomplices as well as to the hijackers. In addition, the use of hijacked aircraft as lethal weapons can be interpreted as a crime against humanity under international law (according to the Statute of the ICC).

Changes in the law of war, human rights law and in other legal domains, have placed individuals, governments and non-governmental organisations under new systems of legal regulation – regulation which, in principle, recasts the legal significance of state boundaries. The regime of liberal international sovereignty entrenches powers and constraints, and rights and duties in international law which – albeit ultimately formulated by states – go beyond the traditional conception of the proper scope and boundaries of states, and can come into conflict, and sometimes contradiction, with national laws. Within this framework, states may forfeit claims to sovereignty, and individuals their right to sovereign protection, if they violate the standards and values embedded in the liberal international order; and such violations no longer become a matter of morality alone. Rather, they become a breach of a legal code, a breach that may call forth the means to challenge, prosecute and rectify it.[7] To this end, a bridge is created between morality and law where, at best, only stepping stones existed before in the era of classic sovereignty. These are transformative changes which alter the form and content of politics nationally, regionally and globally. They signify the enlarging normative reach, extending scope and growing institutionalisation of international legal rules and practices, the beginnings of a 'universal constitutional order' in which the state is no longer the only layer of legal competence to which people have transferred public powers.[8]

In short, boundaries between states are of decreasing legal and moral relevance. Political communities can no longer claim the deep legal and moral significance they once had; they can be judged by general, if not universal, standards. That is to say, they can be scrutinised and appraised in relation to standards which, in principle, apply to each person, each individual, who is held to be equally worthy of concern and respect. Concomitantly, shared membership in a political community, or spatial proximity, is not regarded as a sufficient source of moral privilege.[9]

The political and legal transformations of the last fifty years or so have gone some way toward circumscribing and delimiting political power on a regional and global basis. Several major difficulties remain, nonetheless, at the core of the liberal international regime of sovereignty creating tensions, if not faultlines, at its centre. I shall dwell on just one aspect of these here.

Serious deficiencies can, of course, be documented in the implementation and enforcement of democratic and human rights, and of international law more generally. Despite the development and consolidation of the regime of liberal international sovereignty, massive inequalities of power and economic resources continue to grow. There is an accelerating gap between rich and poor states as well as between peoples in the global economy.[10] The human rights agenda often has a hollow ring. The development of regional trade and investment blocs, particularly the Triad (NAFTA, the EU and Japan), has concentrated economic transactions within and between these areas.[11] The Triad accounts for two-thirds to three-quarters of world economic activity, with shifting patterns of resources across each region. However, one further element of inequality is particularly apparent: a significant proportion of the world's population remains marginal to these networks.[12]

Does this growing gulf in the life circumstances and life chances of the world's population highlight intrinsic limits to the liberal international order, or should this disparity be traced to other phenomena, such as the particularisation of nation-states or the inequalities of regions with their own distinctive cultural, religious and political problems? The latter phenomena are contributors to the disparity between the universal claims of the human rights regime and its often tragically limited impact. But one of the key causes of the gulf lies, in my judgement, elsewhere; in the tangential impact of the liberal international order on the regulation of economic power and market mechanisms. The focus of the liberal international order is on the curtailment of the abuse of political power, not economic power. It has few, if any, systematic means to address sources of power other than the political.[13] Its conceptual resources and leading ideas do not suggest or push toward the pursuit of self-determination and autonomy in the economic domain; they do not seek the establishment of democratic rights and obligations outside of the sphere of the political. Hence, it is hardly a surprise that liberal democracy and flourishing economic inequalities exist side-by-side.

Thus, the complex and differentiated narratives of globalisation point in stark and often contradictory directions. On the one side, there is the dominant tendency of economic globalisation over the last three decades towards a pattern set by the deregulatory, neo-liberal model; an increase in the exit options of corporate and finance capital relative to labour and the state, and an increase in the volatility of market responses, which has exacerbated a growing sense of political uncertainty and risk; and the marked polarisation of global relative economic inequalities (as well as serious doubt as to whether there has been a 'trickle-down' effect to the world's poorest at all). On the other side, there is the significant entrenchment of cosmopolitan values concerning the equal dignity and worth of all human beings; the reconnection of international law and morality; the establishment of regional and global systems of governance; and growing recognition that the public good – whether conceived as financial stability, environmental protection, or global egalitarianism – requires co-ordinated multilateral action if it is to be achieved in the long term.

11 September, war and justice

If 11 September was not a defining moment in human history, it certainly was for today's generations. The terrorist violence was an atrocity of extraordinary proportions. It was a crime against the USA and against humanity; a massive breach of many of the core codes of international law; and an attack on the fundamental principles of freedom, democracy, justice and humanity itself, i.e. those principles which affirm the sanctity of life, the importance of self-determination and of equal rights and liberty.

These principles are not just western principles. Elements of them had their origins in the early modern period in the West, but their validity extends much further than this. For these principles are the basis of a fair, humane and decent society, of whatever religion or cultural tradition. To paraphrase the legal theorist Bruce Ackerman, there is no nation without a woman who yearns for equal rights, no society without a man who denies the need for deference and no developing country without a person who does not wish for the minimum means of subsistence so that they may go about their everyday lives.[14] The principles of freedom, democracy and justice are the basis for articulating and reinforcing the equal liberty of all human beings, wherever they were born or brought up. They are the basis of underwriting the liberty of others, not of obliterating it. Their concern is with the irreducible moral status of each and every person – the acknowledgement of which links directly to the possibility of self-determination and the capacity to make independent choices.[15]

The intensity of the range of responses to the atrocities of 11 September is fully understandable. There cannot be many people in the world who did not experience shock, revulsion, horror, anger and a desire for vengeance, as the Kingsolver passage acknowledges. This emotional range is perfectly natural within the context of the immediate events. But it cannot be the basis for a more considered and wise response, in the short or long term.

The founding principles of our society dictate that we do not overgeneralise our response from one moment and one set of events; that we do not jump to conclusions based on concerns that emerge in one particular country at one moment; and that we do not rewrite and rework international law and governance arrangements from one place – in other words, that we do not think and act over-hastily and take the law into our hands. Clearly, the fight against terror must be put on a new footing. Terrorists must be bought to heel and those who protect and nurture them must be bought to account. Zero tolerance is fully justified in these circumstances. Terrorism negates our most elementary and cherished principles and values. But any defensible, justifiable and sustainable response to 11 September must be consistent with our founding principles and the aspirations of international society for security, law, and the impartial administration of justice – aspirations painfully articulated after the Holocaust and the Second World War – and embedded, albeit imperfectly, in regional and global law and the institutions of global governance. If the means deployed to fight terrorism contradict these principles and achievements, then the emotion of the moment might be satisfied, but our vulnerability will be deepened.

War and bombing were and are one option. President Bush described the attacks of 11 September, and the US led coalition response, as a 'new kind of war'; and indeed the attacks of 11 September can be viewed as a more dramatic version of patterns of violence witnessed during the last decade, in the wars in the Balkans, the Middle East and Africa. These wars are quite different from, for example, the Second World War, as Mary Kaldor explains elsewhere in this volume.

In Western security policy, there is a dangerous gulf between the dominant thinking about security based on 'old wars' – like the Second World War and the Cold War – and the reality in the field. The so-called Revolution in Military Affairs, the development of 'smart' weaponry to fight wars at long distance, the proposals for the National Missile Defense programme, were all predicated on outdated assumptions about the nature of war – the idea that it is possible to protect territory from attacks by outsiders. The language of President Bush, with its emphasis on the defence of the US and of dividing the world between those 'who are with us or against us', tends to reproduce the illusion, drawn from the experience of World War II, that this is simply a war between 'good' states led by the United States and 'bad' states. Such an approach is regrettable and, potentially, very dangerous.

Today, a clear-cut military victory is very difficult to achieve because the advantages of supposedly superior technology have been eroded in many contexts. As the Russians discovered in Afghanistan and Chechnya, the Americans in Vietnam, and the Israelis in the current period, conquering people and territory by military means has become an increasingly problematic form of warfare. These military campaigns have all been lost or suffered serious and continuous setbacks as a result of the stubborn refusal of movements for independence or autonomy to be suppressed; the refusal to meet the deployment of the conventional means of interstate warfare with similar forces which play by the same set of rules; and by the constantly shifting use of irregular or guerrilla forces which sporadically but steadily inflict major casualties on states (whose domestic populations become increasingly anxious and weary). And the risks of using high-tech weapon systems, carpet bombing and other highly destructive means of interstate warfare are very high, to say the least.

An alternative approach is one that counters the strategy of 'fear and hate'. What is needed, as Mary Kaldor and I have argued,[16] is a movement for global, not American, justice and legitimacy, aimed at establishing and extending the rule of law in place of war and at fostering understanding between communities in place of terror. Such a movement must press upon governments and international institutions the importance of three things.

First, there must be a commitment to the rule of law, not the prosecution of war. Civilians of all faiths and nationalities need protection, wherever they live, and terrorists must be captured and brought before an international criminal court, which could be either permanent or modelled on the Nuremberg or Yugoslav war crimes tribunals. The terrorists must be treated as criminals, and not glamorised as military adversaries. This does not preclude internationally sanctioned military action both to arrest suspects and to dismantle terrorist networks – not at all. But such action should always be understood as a robust form of policing, above all as a way of protecting civilians and bringing criminals to trial. Moreover, this type of action must scrupulously preserve both the laws of war and human rights law.

Second, a massive effort has to be undertaken to create a new form of global political legitimacy. This cannot be equated with an occasional or one-off effort to create a new momentum for peace and the protection of human rights in the Middle East. It has to be part of a continuous emphasis in foreign policy year-in, year-out, to promote these aims. Many parts of the world will need convincing that the West's interest in security and human rights for all regions and peoples is not just a product of short-term geo-political or geo-economic interests.

And, finally, there must be a head-on acknowledgement that the ethical and justice issues posed by the global polarisation of wealth, income and power, and with them the huge asymmetries of life chances, cannot be left to markets to resolve. Those who are poorest and most vulnerable, locked into geopolitical situations which have neglected their economic and political claims for generations, will always provide fertile ground for terrorist recruiters. The project of economic globalisation has to be connected to manifest principles of social justice; the latter need to reframe global market activity.

Of course, terrorist crimes of the kind we witnessed on 11 September may often be the work of the simply deranged and the fanatic, and so there can be no guarantee that a more just world will be a more peaceful one in all respects. But if we turn our back on this challenge, there is no hope of ameliorating the social basis of disadvantage often experienced in the poorest and most dislocated countries. Gross injustices, linked to a sense of hopelessness born of generations of neglect, feed anger and hostility. Popular support against terrorism depends upon convincing people that there is a legal and pacific way of addressing their grievances. Without this sense of confidence in public institutions and processes, the defeat of terrorism becomes a hugely difficult task, if it can be achieved at all.

Kant was right: the violent abrogation of law and justice in one place ricochets across the world. We cannot accept the burden of putting justice right in one dimension of life – security – without at the same time seeking to put it right everywhere. A socio-economic order in which whole regions and peoples suffer serious harm and disadvantage independently of their will or consent, will not command widespread support and legitimacy. If the political, social and economic dimensions of justice are separated in the long term – as is the tendency in the global order today – the prospects for a peaceful and civil society will be bleak indeed.

Islam, the Kantian heritage and double standards

The responsibility for the pursuit of justice does not just fall on the West. It is not simply the USA and Europe that must look critically at themselves in the aftermath of 11 September; there is a pressing need for self-examination in parts of Islam as well. The Muslim writer, Ziauddin Sardar, wrote in the aftermath of the attacks:

'To Muslims everywhere I issue this fatwa: any Muslim involved in the planning, financing, training, recruiting, supporting or harbouring of those who commit acts of indiscriminate violence against persons... is guilty of terror and no part of the *ummah*. It is the duty of every Muslim to spare no effort in hunting down, apprehending and bringing such criminals to justice.

If you see something reprehensible, said the Prophet Muhammad, then change it with your hand; if you are not capable of that then use your tongue (speak out against it); and if you are not capable of that then detest it in your heart. The silent Muslim majority must now become vocal.' (Z. Sardar, *Guardian*, 22 September 2001)

Iman Hamza, a noted Islamic teacher, has spoken of the 'deep denial' many Muslims seem to be in. He is concerned that "Islam has been hijacked by a discourse of anger and a rhetoric of rage".[17] The attacks of 11 September appear to have been perpetrated in the name of Islam, albeit a particular version of Islam. It is this version of Islam which must be repudiated by the wider Islamic community, who need to reaffirm the compatibility of Islam with the universal, cosmopolitan principles that put life and the free development of all human beings at their centre.

The fundamental fissure in the Muslim world is between those who want to uphold universal standards, including the standards of democracy and human rights, and want to reform their societies, dislodging the deep connection between religion, culture and politics, and those who are threatened by this and wish to retain and/or restore power to those who represent 'fundamentalist' ideals. The political, economic and cultural challenges posed by the globalisation of (for want of a better short hand) 'modernity' now face the counterforce of the globalisation of radical Islam. This poses many big questions, but one in particular should be stressed; that is, how far and to what extent Islam – and not just the West – has the capacity to confront its own ideologies, double-standards and limitations. Clearly, the escape from dogma and unvindicated authority – the removal of constraints on the public use of reason – has a long way to go, East and West. The Kantian heritage should be accepted across Islam as well.

It would be a mistake to think that this is simply an outsider's challenge to Islam. Islam, like the other great world religions, has incorporated a diverse body of thought and practice. In addition, it has contributed, and accommodated itself, to ideas of religious tolerance, secular political power and human rights. It is particularly in the contemporary period that radical Islamic movements have turned their back on these important historical developments and sought to deny Islam's contribution both to the Enlightenment and the formulation of universal ethical codes. There are many good reasons for doubting the often-expressed western belief that thoughts about justice and democracy have only flourished in the West.[18] Islam is not a unitary or explanatory category.[19] Hence, the call for cosmopolitan values speaks to a vital strain within Islam which affirms the importance of rights and justice.

Concluding reflections

It is useful to return to the passage with which I started this essay. It makes uncomfortable reading because it invites reflection on 11 September in the context of other tragedies and conflict situations, and asks the reader to step outside of the maelstrom of 11 September and put those events in a wider historical and evaluative framework. Uncomfortable as this request is, we have to accept it if we are to find a satisfactory way of making sense of 11 September. To begin with, as the passage suggests, it is important to affirm the irreducible moral status of each and every person and, concomitantly, to reject the view of moral particularists that belonging to a given community limits and determines the moral worth of individuals and the nature of their freedom. At the centre of this kind of thinking is the cosmopolitan view that human well-being is not defined by geographical and cultural locations, that national or ethnic or gender boundaries should not determine the limits of rights or responsibilities for the satisfaction of basic human needs, and that all human beings require equal moral respect and concern. Cosmopolitanism builds on the basic principles of equal dignity, equal respect, and the priority of vital need in its preoccupation with what is required for the autonomy and development of all human beings.

Cosmopolitan principles are not principles for some remote utopia; they are at the centre of significant post-Second World War legal and political developments, from the 1948 UN Declaration of Human Rights to the 1998 adoption of the Statute of the International Criminal Court. Many of these developments were framed against the background of formidable threats to humankind – above all, Nazism, fascism and the Holocaust. The framers of these initiatives affirmed the importance of universal principles, human rights, and the rule of law when there were strong temptations simply to put up the shutters and defend the position of some nations and countries only. The response to 11 September could follow in the footsteps of these achievements and strengthen our multilateral institutions and international legal arrangements; or it could take us further away from these fragile gains towards a world of further antagonisms and divisions – a distinctively uncivil society. We have not yet run out of choices – history is still with us and can be made.

David Held is Graham Wallas Professor of Political Science at the London School of Economics.

Acknowledgement

Two sections of this essay have been adapted from my previous writings. The first section draws on some material developed at much greater length in my 'Law of states, law of peoples', *Legal Theory*, 8.2, 2002, forthcoming. The second section draws on my 'Violence and justice in a global age' and, with Mary Kaldor, on 'What hope for the future? Learning the lessons of the past'. Both these pieces were made available initially through OpenDemocracy.net.

[1] See D. Held and A. McGrew, D. Goldblatt and J. Perraton, (1999) *Global Transformations: Politics, Economics and Culture*, Cambridge: Polity Press, Chaps. 3-5; also D. Held and A. McGrew (eds) (2000) *The Global Transformation Reader*, Cambridge: Polity Press, Chap. 25.

[2] See J. Vincent (1992) 'Modernity and universal human rights', pp.269-92, in A. McGrew and P. Lewis (eds), *Global Politics*, Cambridge: Polity Press.

[3] A. Cassese (1988) *Violence and Law in the Modern Age*, Cambridge: Polity Press, p.132.

[4] C/f J. Crawford (1995) 'Prospects for an international criminal court', in M. D. A. Freeman and R. Halson (eds), *Current Legal Problems 1995*, 48, pt 2, collected papers, Oxford: Oxford University Press; J. Dugard (1997) 'Obstacles in the way of an international criminal court', Cambridge Law Journal, 56; M. Weller (1997) 'The reality of the emerging universal constitutional order: putting the pieces together', *Cambridge Review of International Studies*, Winter/Spring.

[5] C. Chinkin (1998) 'International law and human rights', in T. Evans (ed.), *Human Rights Fifty Years On: A Reappraisal*, Manchester: Manchester University Press, pp.118-9.

[6] See below; and see for a fuller account D. Held (2002) 'Law of states, law of peoples', *Legal Theory*, 8, 2.

[7] See J. Habermas (1999) 'Bestialität und humanität', *Die Zeit*, 18, April.

[8] J. Crawford and S. Marks (1998) 'The global democracy deficit: an essay on international law and its limits', p.2, in Archibugi et al. (eds) (1998); M. Weller (1997) 'The reality of the emerging universal constitutional order: putting the pieces together', *Cambridge Review of International Studies*, Winter/Spring, p.45

[9] C. Beitz (1998) 'Philosophy of international relations', in the Routledge Encyclopedia of

Philosophy, London: Routledge; T. Pogge (1989) *Realizing Rawls*, Ithaca, N.Y.: Cornell University Press; also (1994a) 'Cosmopolitanism and sovereignty', in C. Brown (ed.) (1994); also (1994b) 'An egalitarian law of peoples', *Philosophy and Public Affairs*, 23, 3; B. Barry (1999) 'Statism and nationalism: a cosmopolitan critique', in I. Shapiro and L. Brilmayer (eds), *Global Justice*, New York: New York University Press; see also below.

[10] UNDP (1999) Globalization with a Human Face: Human Development Report 1999, New York: Oxford University Press.

[11] G. Thompson (2000) 'Economic globalization?', in D. Held (ed.), *A Globalizing World?*, London: Routledge.

[12] See T. Pogge (1999) 'Economic justice and national borders', *Revision*, 22, 2; D. Held and A. McGrew (eds) (2000) *The Global Transformation Reader*, Cambridge: Polity Press.

[13] D. Held (1995) Democracy and the Global Order: From the Modern State to Cosmopolitan Governance, Cambridge: Polity Press.

[14] B. Ackerman (1994) 'Political liberalisms', *Journal of Philosophy*, 91, 7; see also A. Sen (1992) *Inequality Reexamined*, Oxford: Clarendon Press; and A. Sen (1999) *Development as Freedom*, Oxford: Oxford University Press.

[15] See M. Nussbaum (1997) 'Kant and cosmopolitanism', in J. Bohman and M. Lutz-Bachmann (eds) (1997).

[16] D. Held and M. Kaldor (2001). 'What hope for the future? Learning the lessons from the past', OpenDemocracy.net.

[17] Cit. in H. Young (2001) 'It may not be PC to say', *Guardian*, 9 October 2001.

[18] A. Sen (1996) 'Humanity and citizenship', in J. Cohen (ed.), *For Love of Country*, Boston: Beacon Press, p.118.

[19] See F. Halliday (1996), *Islam and the Myth of Confrontation*, London: I.B.Tauris.

8 Reform of the Global Institutional Architecture[1]

Fernando Henrique Cardoso

The attacks of 11 September 2001 were an act of aggression against humanity. Terrorism undermines the very principles of civilised behaviour. It fosters fear and threatens the security of all countries.

The charter of the United Nations acknowledges the right of member states to act in self-defence. This is not in doubt. But let us keep in mind that the struggle against terrorism cannot rely exclusively on self-defence measures or on the use of military force by individual countries. In 1945 the United Nations committed itself to the task of laying the foundations for peace and the protection of future generations against the scourge of war. War always takes a heavy human toll: a cost in lives cut short and in lives overtaken by fear and flight. This underscores the responsibility of terrorists for what is happening today. Brazil hopes that, notwithstanding these circumstances, humanitarian assistance efforts in Afghanistan will not be frustrated. Moreover we will, within our possibilities, welcome refugees wishing to settle in our country.

Though obvious, it warrants repeating that the struggle against terrorism is not, and must never become, a clash between civilisations, much less between religions. Not one of the civilisations that have enriched and humanised our planet can say that it has not known, within its own historical experience, episodes of violence and terror.

Around the world, problems related to crime, drug abuse and trafficking, and money laundering are evils related to terrorism, which must be eradicated. I wish to call for a world-wide public awareness campaign to make drug users realise that, even if inadvertently, they are helping finance terrorism. If we are to stem the flow of resources to the terrorist networks spreading death and destruction, it is crucial that drug use in our societies be drastically curtailed.

Furthermore, we must not allow differences in national tax regimes to be used as an instrument to foster capital flight, to the detriment of economic development, or to help finance organised crime, including terrorist actions. If the existence of tax havens is inseparable from these problems, then tax havens should not exist. We must put an end to these safe harbours of corruption and terror, towards which some governments have up to now been complacent.

It is only natural that, after 11 September, issues of international security should be given high priority. Yet terrorism must not be allowed to stifle the debate on cooperation and other issues of global interest. The road to the future requires that the forces of globalisation be harnessed in the pursuit of lasting peace, a peace sustained not by fear, but rather by the willing acceptance by all countries of a just international order. On this theme, I have sought to mobilise numerous world leaders. Brazil wishes to play its part to ensure that the world does not squander the opportunities that are contained in the present crisis.

Let us focus on our fundamental imperative of promoting development. The process of globalisation is tainted by an undeniable sense of unease. I am not referring to the ideological disquiet of those who oppose globalisation on principle. Neither have I in mind those who reject the very notion of universal values, which inspire freedom and the respect for human rights. Rather, what I have in mind is the fact that globalisation has not lived up to its promises. There is a governance deficit in the international sphere, and it results from a democratic deficit. Globalisation will only be sustainable if enriched by a sense of justice. Our motto should be 'globalisation in solidarity' rather than the asymmetrical globalisation of today.

In the field of trade, it is high time multilateral negotiations translated into greater access for goods from developing countries into the more prosperous markets. We must ensure that the new round of multilateral trade negotiations indeed turns out to be a 'development round'. To this end, it is crucial that priority be awarded to those issues most conducive to the dismantling of protectionist practices and barriers in developed countries. Brazil has taken the lead in negotiations to ensure greater market access and better humanitarian conditions in the fight against diseases. We will seek to strike a balance between the requirements of patent rights and the imperative of providing care to those most in need. We favour market practices and the protection of intellectual property, but not at the cost of human lives. This is a point that must be carefully defined: life must prevail over material interests.

The Bretton Woods institutions must be revamped if they are to respond to the challenges of the twenty-first century. The IMF must be allotted greater resources so as to allow it to function as lender of last resort. For their part, the World Bank and regional banks must be given a more active part in fostering economic growth and development. The volatility of international capital flows must be contained and the financial system made more predictable and less crisis-prone, as proposed by the G-20. Similarly, although measures such as the 'Tobin Tax' present practical difficulties, it should be possible to look into better and less compulsory alternatives. These issues should be given special attention at the UN Conference on the Financing of Development, to be held this year in Monterrey.

We must also envisage practical forms of cooperation to alleviate the tragedy of AIDS, above all in Africa. How long will the world remain indifferent to the plight of those who might yet be saved from disease, deprivation and exclusion?

The 20th century came to an end amid a growing sense of global citizenship and universally shared values. Brazil is determined to forge ahead in this direction. The International Criminal Court will be a historic victory for the cause of human rights. The protection of the environment and sustainable development are equally pressing challenges of our time. The process of climate change has been scientifically ascertained as a fact, but it is not unstoppable.

What the future holds depends on what we do today, in particular as concerns the Kyoto Protocol. Brazil warmly welcomes the successful outcome of the Marrakesh meeting, which is a decisive step towards controlling and eventually reversing the warming of the atmosphere. I call for the prompt ratification of the Kyoto Protocol.

Recent events in New York, Washington and elsewhere clearly demonstrate the grave threat from weapons of mass destruction. No matter the nature of the menace – bacteriological, such as anthrax, chemical or nuclear – there is no alternative to disarmament and non-proliferation. It is an ethical imperative that science and technology must not be turned into a weapon in the hands of the irresponsible. This requires the active and legitimate involvement of the United Nations in the control, destruction and eradication of these arsenals.

Just as it supported the creation of the state of Israel, Brazil today calls for concrete measures towards the setting-up of a Palestinian state that is democratic, united and economically viable. The right of the Palestinian people to self-determination and the respect for the existence of Israel as a sovereign, free and secure state are essential if the Middle East is to rebuild its future in peace. This is a moral debt owed by the international community. It is a task that must not be postponed.

It is equally urgent that a lasting solution be found to the conflict in Angola, which deserves the opportunity to get back on the road to development. This is the same future that Brazil wishes for East Timor, which we hope will soon take its rightful place in the United Nations General Assembly as a sovereign state.

A strong and agile United Nations is required if the world is to respond to increasingly complex problems. The United Nations will only be strengthened if the General Assembly becomes more active, more respected, and if the Security Council becomes more representative. Its composition should no longer be a reflection of arrangements among the victors of a conflict that took place over 50 years ago, and for whose triumph Brazilian soldiers gave their blood in the glorious campaigns in Italy. Brazil joins those who appeal for more democracy in international relations in calling for the enlargement of the Security Council. Common sense requires the inclusion, in the category of permanent members, of those developing countries with the necessary credentials to exercise the responsibilities that today's world imposes upon them.

By the same token, Brazil believes that an enlargement of the G8 is called for in view of the transformations the world is presently undergoing. It is no longer admissible to restrict to such a limited group of countries the discussion of issues pertaining to globalisation and its inevitable impact on the political and economic life of emerging economies.

An international order that is more just and based on solidarity will only come about through a concerted effort on the part of the community of nations. This is too precious a goal to be left to the vagaries of market forces or to the whims of power politics. We do not aspire to a world government, but we cannot sidestep the obligation to ensure that international relations are not left rudderless, but reflect the legitimate aspirations of the majority. The nefarious shadow of terrorism points to what can be expected if we do not enhance mutual understanding among peoples.

The United Nations was created under the sign of dialogue, a dialogue among sovereign states that are subject to free nations, whose peoples actively participate in national decision-making. With their help, we can ensure that the 21st century will not be a time of fear, but rather of the flourishing of a freer humanity, in peace with itself, and rationally oriented towards the building of an international order that is acceptable to all peoples and that provides a guiding framework for states at the global level. This is the challenge of the twenty-first century. Let us face it inspired by the grand vision of the founding fathers of the United Nations, who dreamed of a pluralistic world, founded on peace, solidarity, tolerance and reason, which is the ultimate source of the rule of law.

Fernando Henrique Cardoso is President of the Federative Republic of Brazil.

[1] This essay is based on a speech delivered to the United Nations General Assembly on 10 November, 2001.

9 An Equal Partner: Europe's Role in the World Order

Malcolm Chalmers

In the aftermath of 11 September, as governments throughout Europe placed their security forces on alert against possible new terrorist attacks, the transatlantic tensions that had characterised the first months of the Bush Presidency were put into perspective. Differences remained, of course, over many issues (ranging from arms control to combating climate change). They will continue to be the focus for fierce debate between and within countries. But both sides of the Atlantic are united by the realisation that differences of emphasis and priority cannot get in the way of co-operation against a common and pressing threat.

The US administration initially gained credit in Europe by the careful and proportionate nature of its military action, its refusal simply to lash out in anger, and its emphasis on the need to target those responsible for the atrocities and those who harbour them. Public concern in Europe over the humanitarian consequences of a prolonged bombing campaign did begin to grow, and was fuelled by pessimistic military warnings that the campaign could last many months. But the sudden collapse of Taliban resistance in the major cities, and the allies' success in largely eliminating al-Qaida's network in Afghanistan, took the wind out of the sails of the war's critics.

European governments were also pleased that efforts to construct a broad anti-terrorist coalition had led the US to revisit its relationships with both Russia and China, easing concerns that unilateral US actions (for example the decision to withdraw from the ABM Treaty with Russia, which currently limits the testing of anti-ballistic missile defences) might lead to new international tensions. It remains to be seen whether Europe will remain supportive of US priorities in the 'war against terrorism' in coming months, especially if the US seeks to extend military action to other countries (such as Iraq) which have not been directly linked to the 11 September atrocities. But such proposals are opposed by some within the Administration, who fear their destabilising consequences for the region. At the time of writing, it is unclear what action, if any, will be taken with respect to those countries identified as 'the axis of evil'.

The period of intense warfare that began on 7 October was dominated by the US's ability to unleash massive air strikes on the Taliban's infrastructure and, latterly, its front line troops (although allied special forces, including those of the UK, also appear to have played a significant role). With the fall of Mazir and Kabul to the Northern Alliance in November, however, European forces began to play a more visible role, much as they had done in Kosovo. At the same time, European governments declared their willingness to make substantial contributions to long-term post-war reconstruction in Afghanistan. At the time of writing, it is too early to know whether these promises will be fulfilled, or indeed whether the conditions can be created in which they can be. Yet in whatever direction the crisis now goes, it has already served to emphasise just how far European thinking about the deployment of military force has moved in the last few years. It is remarkable enough that both the UK and France have been prepared to deploy significant numbers of their elite troops in Kabul and Mazir to provide security for humanitarian relief and, perhaps, wider support for political stabilisation. It is in some ways even more noteworthy that countries such as Germany and Italy have been willing to make substantial military commitments, overturning past inhibitions and (in the case of Germany) risking defeat in a parliamentary vote of confidence.

The evolution of European defence thinking that has made possible such commitments began with the EU's humiliation in the Balkan wars of the early 1990s. Unwilling to undertake coercive action against

Serbian aggression without US leadership, Europe's leading states stood by while Croatia and Bosnia saw escalating warfare and atrocities. Eventually, neither the US nor Europe was prepared to stand by any longer, and NATO imposed a fragile peace on the region, first in Bosnia then in Kosovo. Today, there is widespread, if reluctant, acceptance that NATO military forces could be in the region for many years to come. Talk of an 'exit strategy' has gone, and instead the focus is on a 'strategy for entry' – creating the conditions under which the region can be fully integrated into European institutions.

As the priority has shifted to post-war stabilisation, the main responsibility for providing military forces in the former Yugoslavia has been taken by Europeans. The US presence seems likely to decline further in future, in the light of increasing demands elsewhere. But Europe seems certain to be there for the long haul. And the realisation that Europe has to be prepared to do more for itself in defence terms, and that sometimes it may have to operate when the US chooses not to be involved, proved the key factor in the 1999 decision to adopt a European Security and Defence Policy. It is still too early to assess the effectiveness of the new institutional mechanisms being created. Perhaps the most important changes are, however, taking place at national level. As the response to the Afghan crisis has demonstrated, there is a real convergence of approach between European states that bodes well for future co-operation.

Yet European governments are under no illusions about the limits to their military power compared to that of the United States. Although they spend, collectively, around half as much on defence as the US, the countries of the European Union can only muster a small fraction of the US's ability to project military power worldwide. Europe will therefore continue to rely on the US in future crises – including crises which might involve terrorist attacks on targets in Europe.

The capability gap between the US and Europe is partly a consequence of the way in which European governments choose to spend their defence budgets. But it is also a result of the gap in spending levels, a gap that seems certain to grow in the wake of September 11. While some additional investments in priority levels may now be made, no European government is considering increases in defence spending comparable to those planned by the Pentagon.

By contrast, European leaders are markedly more willing than their US counterparts to argue the case for increased resources to be spent on non-military responses to conflict. Tony Blair, in particular, has emphasised that the international community has failed to do enough to address wider problems of underdevelopment and marginalisation. Gordon Brown, the UK's finance minister, has followed this up by arguing that a doubling of OECD aid budgets will be needed if the UN's ambition of halving the proportion of people in poverty by 2015 is to be achieved.

Even if there is broad agreement on common objectives, therefore, the US and the European states are offering a very different mix of contributions to the pursuit of those objectives. The US will continue to contribute disproportionately to defence, and seems certain to consolidate its position as the world's single military superpower and ultimate security guarantor when other means have failed. By contrast, the primary responsibility for leadership in providing other 'international public goods' will, very often, fall on Europe.

Such a 'division of labour' need not be unhelpful, drawing as it does on the comparative strengths of each country. But it cannot be taken to extremes. If a sense of common purpose is to be maintained, and with it a commitment to seek common policies, it will remain important that all countries (or as many as possible) do something – whether it is contributing to the Afghanistan aid consortium, the NATO military force in Kosovo or the UN's budget. Effective international action often requires leadership – the willingness of one country, or group of countries, to take primary responsibility for action. But it also requires broad participation if it is to be sustained and the potential for division is to be avoided.

Where then can European countries make their most effective contributions, in the light of the comparative advantages they possess, and the problems that they face?

Close to home

Sixty years ago, Europe was a devastated continent, suffering the consequences of ten years of all-out war in the space of three decades. Europe's remarkable recovery from that period, and its creation of a lasting peace between its competing nation-states, is one of the greatest achievements of the late 20th century.

The creation of this European 'security community' has many causes, including the spread of democracy, economic interdependence and the glue provided by a common external threat. Not least, it involved the development of unique new organisations, the EU and NATO, that have institutionalised co-operation, consolidated democracy, and promoted economic integration. In time, the benefits of this 'security community' were extended to Spain, Portugal and Greece, which had previously suffered from right-wing dictatorship and economic underdevelopment. But EU membership played a crucial role in overcoming these legacies; and significant progress has been made in achieving economic 'convergence' with Europe's richest states.

The objective of extending Western Europe's 'security community' to the rest of the continent is now at the heart of the EU's foreign policy. Ten states (including Poland) now seem to be on track to join the EU by 2004 or 2005. The Czech Republic, Hungary and Poland are already NATO members, and a significant further NATO enlargement is on the cards, and may be agreed this year. After what has seemed to be an interminable delay during the 1990s, it now seems likely that much of Central and Eastern Europe will be inside both NATO and the EU within the next few years.

The implications of EU enlargement, in particular, will be profound. For a decade, the countries of central and eastern Europe have been supplicants, having to fulfil hundreds of conditions, and implement thousands of pages of EU laws and regulations, in order to qualify for membership. Once they do become members, however, this relationship will be transformed. Despite the changes in voting rules agreed at Nice, the new members will have considerable powers within the EU, and will be able, in particular, to argue that financial transfers within the EU (through the regional aid and agricultural budgets) should reflect their relative poverty. The result, at the 2006 budget review, is almost certain to be a big increase in net EU budget contributions from existing member states. Seen in the context of the gains, both strategic and economic, that enlargement will bring, these costs are manageable. But national politicians will be under considerable pressure not to sacrifice their own benefits, the Common Agricultural Policy for France, regional aid for Spain, and so on. It will require considerable political skill on the part of EU leaders, therefore, to manage the burden-sharing implications of enlargement.

Even as EU countries prepare to meet the costs of enlargement, moreover, they will also be facing the implications of their commitment to supporting economic and political development in south-eastern Europe. The prospects for graduation to full EU membership in this region varies, with some countries (such as Bulgaria and Croatia) being real possibilities before 2010. Others, especially those which have suffered most from conflict, may take much longer. In total, the costs of these commitments in terms of military forces as well as financial aid are likely to remain substantial. Again, however, these investments will be essential if this part of the continent is to be stabilised and rebuilt.

Not least, the momentum created by eastern enlargement will increase pressure, especially from Poland and the Baltic states, for the EU to take on an active role on its new eastern frontier; that is, in Belarus, Ukraine and Russia. The aftermath of September 11 has seen the creation of a major opportunity to put relations between Russia and the West on a new footing. The fierce Russian antagonism towards NATO that was evident during the Kosovo war now seems forgotten. And

President Putin clearly believes in the need for a fundamental reorientation of Russian foreign policy towards cooperation with the US and NATO.

It is far too early to tell whether this shift can be sustained, given the widespread unease that appears to exist amongst influential Russian elites. There is also some danger that the West may raise Russian expectations too high, for example, by appearing to hold out the prospect of early membership of the WTO or NATO. Nevertheless, a major opportunity for permanent improvement in relations may exist. Already, it seems likely that closer Russia/NATO cooperation will now make NATO membership for the Baltic states possible.

While the agenda of relations with Russia remains dominated by strategic arms control and military access to Central Asia, the US will continue to play a leading role in exploring possible cooperation. Insofar as military factors begin to play a less dominant role in Russia's relations with the Western world, however, Europe's relative importance as an interlocutor will increase. Europe has most to fear from developments in Russia: not because of the threat of military attack, but because of the spillover effects of environmental and economic collapse. And Europe therefore has most to gain from a stable Russia, able to contain infectious disease, curb organised crime, and tackle the dangers posed by its rotting nuclear-military complex. Not least, given uncertainty over the long-term future of states such as Saudi Arabia, Europe has much to gain from secure access to Russian energy supplies. If the prospect of Russian membership of the World Trade Organisation ever becomes realistic, moreover, European companies may have most to gain from opening up its markets to foreign investment and competition.

The wider world

The challenges involved in creating security within Europe are themselves formidable. But the Afghan crisis has reinforced the need for the EU and its leaders to develop a foreign policy that looks beyond their immediate neighbourhood. The UK Government has set forward an ambitious programme for increasing its provision of overseas development assistance (ODA), as part of a wider set of measures designed to tackle global underdevelopment. But UK Government commitments have not been matched by similar increases in other major European states; and it remains to be seen whether the crisis in Afghanistan will encourage a new sense of urgency.

US military power will remain an essential part of the response to the problems created by global terrorism and the proliferation of weapons of mass destruction. When they support US military action outside Europe, EU states will want the capability to show solidarity with forces of their own. In contrast to the US, however, EU states are not seeking the ability to fight a major war outside their continent independently. Such a capability will remain the sole preserve of the US, and European policy will have to live with this continuing reality.

At the same time, European governments will have comparative strengths in dealing with the problems of humanitarian assistance, post-conflict reconstruction and long-term development assistance. The record of European aid donors, both bilateral and EU, is mixed; and it is as important to improve the quality of ODA as it will be to increase its volume. Nevertheless, European states are probably better placed than the US (and probably also than Japan) to take the lead in efforts in this field.

Most European governments (with the honourable exceptions of Denmark, the Netherlands, Norway and Sweden) have consistently failed to meet the UN's target of spending 0.7% of their national income on overseas aid. Their record looks good, therefore, only compared to that of the US. It is difficult to make even this claim when one examines the EU's unwillingness to open key markets to poor country exports. European agricultural protectionism remains particularly strong. The opening of a new round of trade talks provides an opportunity to focus the next round of trade liberalisation on the needs of developing countries, with Chinese accession to membership adding to the pressure for a shift in emphasis away from US/EU dominance. If European leaders are serious in their commitment to tackling global poverty, this will be one of the key areas where it could be demonstrated.

Global community

Some of the most difficult issues that threaten to divide the US from Europe concern the future of international agreements and organisations. The EU is, by its very nature, a strong believer in international agreement, and its member states are accustomed to having their sovereignty limited (through common EU policies) in areas such as control of currency that are the prerogative of national governments in other parts of the world. The US political elite, by contrast, remains deeply suspicious of encroachments on its sovereignty: a suspicion that borders on paranoia in sections of the Republican Party. That is why, so often, the US has been in a minority of one (at least amongst rich-world states) in rejecting key international treaties and agreements, from the Kyoto protocols on combating global warming to the International Criminal Court. Not least, President Bush's administration has made clear its deep suspicion of arms control. It has failed to ratify the Comprehensive Nuclear Test Ban Treaty and has withdrawn from the Anti-Ballistic-Missile Treaty. It has also blocked agreement on a verification protocol to the Biological Weapons Convention, to the intense annoyance of EU governments. Even when agreement was reached on strategic arms reductions, as in the November summit with President Putin, President Bush rejected the suggestion that the reductions be formally codified. The impression given has been that, ideally, the US administration would be much happier without any arms control treaties at all.

At the same time, however, many in the US are willing to be convinced that some agreements, at least, are in its interests. After all, the US shares a widespread interest in preventing biological weapons proliferation, even if it would prefer a different treaty from the one that has been negotiated. It is coming to realise that it too will suffer from global warming, and that it therefore has an interest in ensuring that the costs of tackling this problem are shared internationally. The US continues to benefit substantially from the rule-based international trade order, without which all might suffer from a protectionist spiral. Since 11 September, US leaders have too come to realise that international regimes also have a role to play in monitoring suspect financial transactions and in promoting anti-terrorist collaboration.

Given the uncertain level of support for multilateralism in today's US, however, European governments have often had to accept that they may have to do more – and act first – if international organisations and regimes are to be created and then allowed to grow. This realisation was the key to the UN funding deal reached in December 2000, when EU governments agreed to a significant reduction in the US contribution (to a proportion of its national income well below that of EU member states) in return for assurances that the US would be committed to actually paying its contributions in future. It has also been important in the recent agreement to go ahead with binding international agreement on greenhouse gas emissions without the participation of the US. The limits agreed upon are modest, and European self-congratulation can be overdone. Even so, Europe's willingness to take a lead in this area, at some modest economic cost, holds out the possibility that formal pollution limits can be expanded in future to include not only the US, but also major developing industrialised countries such as China and India. In the meantime, EU action has helped encourage companies and scientists to believe there is a future market for the environmentally-friendly technologies that will be essential if the world is to combat the threat of global warming.

Conclusion
In the aftermath of 11 September, the US and EU are united in pursuit of common objectives. Yet they each bring their own distinct capabilities to this common effort. As in the Cold War, the US's comparative advantage lies, most of all, in military capabilities that no

other power on earth can match. But European countries also have contributions that they are particularly well-qualified to make: expanding Europe's security community, aiding post-conflict reconstruction and providing humanitarian assistance, strengthening global multilateralism. Effective international cooperation requires that national efforts, military, economic or political, be co-ordinated and that all key members of an international community contribute something to the common endeavour. But co-operation is often most effective when one or more countries are willing to take a lead. Atlantic cooperation can be strengthened by the recognition that such a 'division of labour' exists, and can usefully be developed.

Malcolm Chalmers is Professor of International Politics, University of Bradford, and Senior Consulting Fellow at the International Institute for Strategic Studies, London. He is author of *Sharing Security: The Political Economy of Burdensharing*, Palgrave, 2000

PART IV

International Security Post-11 September

10 Security and Counter-Terrorism

Ehud Barak

After 11 September 2001, nothing about terror can ever be taken for granted, or regarded as inconceivable or unthinkable. We live in a condition of fundamental uncertainty, and we do well to re-examine our knowledge of the threat that we face.

What is the terrorist web? A few dozen outlaw organisations, the strands loosely and flexibly interacting with each other. Where are their hiding places? They are deployed in dozens of states, but less than ten are sponsoring and hosting them knowingly and deliberately.

There is a symbiosis between hosting states and terror organisations, and this, plus the interaction among them, joins with the drug traffickers to form a new evil empire. Afghanistan is now the number one producer of opium and heroin and Lebanon is also very high on the list. The terrorists and money-launderers funnel private and state contributions and so-called charity dollars around the world to pay for faked passports and transportation. They slip weapons into diplomatic bags. They exploit cyberspace and the e-world, including e-trade and the derivatives markets. They are skilfully using encryption and ciphering equipment of a very high level of sophistication. And they are remarkably skilled in identifying cracks in standard operating procedures for security or immigration.

We have to deal with them in the same way that out forefathers dealt with piracy on the high seas. Namely, every pirate vessel was a target. No port was allowed to harbour them, or provision them with fresh water or food. And whoever broke the rules was automatically isolated from the rest of the world. It took less than 20 years to achieve a sea change.

Today's radical militant Muslim terrorists are pirates of a different kind. They are not out for material gain, but for the spiritual and material destruction of our civilisation. A deeply entrenched animosity towards the West and the US as its leading power and symbol is transformed into a readiness to launch full scale unlimited terror attacks on our peoples, our economy, and our very existence.

Their initial objective is to root out the US presence and influence from the Arabian peninsula, and to overthrow the regimes in that region. Osama bin Laden was deported from Saudi Arabia in 1991 after threatening Allied troops there during the Gulf War. He later declared that he would fight for the Iraqis and Bosnians, but his obsession is to drive the Americans out and turn Saudi Arabia into a militant, radical, terrorist state.

And the obsession then moves on to the destruction of Israel – on driving the Jewish people into the sea. We would stand with America in this crisis, as we always have, for reasons of shared ideals. But we also stand together because we share a fundamental interest in defeating Osama bin Laden's evil design. The West is not hated by the terrorists because it supports Israel. It is the other way around: Israel is hated because it is perceived as an outpost of democratic values and the western way of life.

The radical militant Islam terror groups draw encouragement from the successes of Khomeini in Iran, the Mujaheedin in Afghanistan, as well as from Saddam's ability to survive the Gulf War. They tend to ignore their failures. They assassinated President Sadat, but failed to shake President Mubarak's regime and come to power in Egypt. They failed in Syria, where President Asad crushed them in Al Hama in 1982, bombing half the city into rubble and killing some 20,000 people.

Radical militant Islam is unique in its repeated use of suicide attackers. There is a deeply distorted psychological element in this perversion of Islamic teaching. The spiritual leaders who are manipulating the future suiciders do not really believe the fable they tell about the chair at the table of the prophet and the 72 black-eyed virgins who are waiting for a 'shaheed' in heaven as soon as they die. These false prophets do not become suicide bombers themselves, nor do they send their own sons on such a final mission.

This kind of terror cannot be defeated without determined patience, strategic goals and tactical flexibility. You have to think and act, not by the book, but 'out of the box': open-eyed, your mind free from any dogma or conventional wisdom. The approach must be systematic: intensive worldwide intelligence-gathering; a wide operational and logistical deployment; economic sanctions and no softness in applying them; diplomatic ultimatums and no backing down from them.

Beyond these, a systematic battle will require:

- Fully streamlined global immigration rules and procedures

- Internationally co-ordinated anti-money laundering legislation and updated rules for the transfer of money and other financial assets

- Significant, though legally authorised, disruptions of the privacy of individuals to enable eavesdropping and the penetration of hard disks, apartments, bank accounts and clandestine cells of suspected terrorist individuals or groups

- Reassessment of a generation-old American practice, which did not allow pre-emptive strikes against terrorists and terror operatives

- A crash research-and-development programme to counter biological and chemical threats

- Major improvements in airport and flight security; in Israel for example, for over 30 years, we have been flying with armed undercover air marshals on every flight. For 30 years now, we have also been flying domestic and international flights with pilots in closed cockpits behind two different bullet-proof doors. The system costs some $10,000

- For 30 years the names and personal data of each and every passenger have been screened in advance before check-in. Moreover, no Israeli aeroplane would take off if even one person who checked his baggage in did not show up for boarding.

I believe that all these practices and perhaps more safeguards should and will be adopted now by the US and other Western authorities. A modified version should be implemented for theatres, sporting events and at sites of major physical or symbolic value.

As we improve our defences, we must also win an offensive battle, which must be fought in stages, with a clear strategic plan. The military action in Afghanistan has set an example for other terrorist groups and hosting regimes in regard to the price that has to be paid for standing on the wrong side of the divide. The Afghan people were never a target – just the Taliban regime and Osama bin Laden. Therefore we must sustain an international effort to provide help for Afghan refugees as well as aid for the poor in Afghanistan. A major effort should be invested in avoiding the war becoming Christianity versus Islam, or the West versus Islam. Many Arab and Muslim regimes are genuinely interested in getting rid of radical Islamic terror, which threatens their long-term survival. Rooting out the Saudi regime and other pragmatic rulers is the number one priority for Osama bin Laden (for example, the letter that was left by the assassin of President Sadat, a terrorist named Al-Islambouli, included some twenty reasons; Egypt's peace with Israel was mentioned only at the end: it was number nineteen. Reason number one was the disrespect shown towards young female students when authorities ordered them to uncover their faces for identification before entering university exams.

The coalition will change and develop from stage to stage. This also applies to the roles that different countries will be called upon to play. For example, after the first stage, Pakistan may find itself under pressure from allies to deal with eliminating terrorist spin-offs that fuel conflict with India in Kashmir. We must do all we can to avoid a nuclear confrontation in the Indian subcontinent.

Israel strongly supports the anti-terrorist coalition, yet we face a dilemma: how, on the one hand, to avoid pushing ourselves into the spearhead of the effort, if only to avoid alienating moderate Arabs, like Egypt and Jordan, from joining. At the same time, how to avoid the emergence of a double standard if terrorist groups like Hamas, Islamic Jihad and Hezbollah or even active terrorist elements of the PLO are left off terror lists – not just tactically, at the beginning, but all along the way. We believe that all terrorist groups as well as all host regimes including Syria, Lebanon and the Palestinian Authority should be compelled to leave their terror behind them.

The 11 September attacks have created a major historical earthquake. The energy has been accumulated over a long period, but once released a series of shock waves will follow before the situation stabilises once again. The whole deployment of the tectonic plates of the geopolitical map will be shifted and, along with the dangers, there are new and significant opportunities, not least with Russia and China. Russia has a vital interest in the defeat of the new forms of terror that hits it in Chechnya and which exploded in Moscow and Minsk. President Putin fully understands that the only prospect of leading Russia out of a long-term economic mess lies in economic partnership with the West. I believe he might be ready to go very far in cooperating with the anti-terror war. Building on this foundation, we can also envision new cooperation against nuclear and missile technology proliferation to counter the common threat from rogue states. Russia may ask for a face-saving formula that will present this as a 'marriage of equals' – for example, better mutual coordination on the missile defence initiative and consultation in advance about expanding NATO eastwards and about the nature of the future world order. China has its own reasons to regard the defeat of terrorism as a matter of real national interest. That nation has a huge minority population including some 60 million Muslims – many of them in the Western Province – and Muslim terror is already spreading into China.

The choice of Beijing as the site of the 2008 Olympic games and the significance of the event in Chinese eyes as a world recognition of China's importance, means that China has a second compelling reason for seeing the anti-terror war successfully concluded by then. As a result of 11 September, China can now be seen by the United States not as an arch-rival, but as a potential future ally against the real enemy – Osama bin Laden and the world-wide web of terrorism. This is an important opportunity for China – and for the West – and we must act on both sides to make sure it is not lost.

As for India and Pakistan, where I spoke earlier of the danger, we also have a new and historic moment of opportunity. The conflict is 55 years old and has roots that go back hundreds of years. Now, with creative diplomacy and new financial support now the Taliban are removed, a joint effort by a triumphant coalition, carried out by the UN and supported by the US along with Europe, Russia and China, could dramatically reduce the prospect of renewed war in Kashmir and the even graver risks of a nuclear showdown.

Finally, there may be an opportunity – not immediately, but eventually – to revive the peace process between Israel and the Palestinians. I believe that at a later stage, assuming that Arafat will finally be ready to arrest Islamic Jihad, Hamas suicide, and other terror operatives – and order an end to violence by his own people there may be a real possibility of resuming negotiations based on Camp David principles, under the auspices of a victorious US and backed by more confident Arab moderate regimes that no longer fear the Osama bin Ladens.

We are in the opening days of an epic struggle that will shape our future, determine the world of our children, and define a new global landscape where democracy can spread, freedom will flourish, and stability will be renewed. As human beings as well as out of self-interest, we have to develop a world sense of a community, a community of nations which honestly respect and care about each other, ready to act on a global basis to lift up other people's children as well as our own – and willing to commit ourselves, once we have won the great and moral battle against terror, to achieve the great moral imperative of social justice. However long, and however resource-demanding, we must act to close the gaps in living conditions and reach out to help the half and more of humankind that has been left behind.

This message, if pronounced loud and clear, and heard across the planet, will help us win this present war and bring tranquillity and equilibrium. Neither effort will be swift or easy. As John Kennedy said at another turning-point, during the Cuban missile crisis "the path we have chosen is full of hazards, as all paths are – but it is the one most consistent with our character and courage." Now, in 2001, the great challenge comes to our generation to free the world from the new tyranny of terror – and then to deliver a new birth of freedom for peoples everywhere.

Ehud Barak is former Prime Minister of Israel.

11 Order out of Chaos:
The Challenge of Failed States

Jack Straw

While we may still be too close to the events of 11 September to begin to form a long-term historical view, it is already clear that the terrorist atrocities in the United States marked a turning point in world affairs. Few events in global history have so completely galvanised the international system into action in so short a time. The fall of the Berlin Wall and the collapse of the Soviet empire may have been one. Yet if the main challenge throughout the 20th century came from states with too much power, the chief problem of the 21st may be states with too little.

After the mass murder in the heart of Manhattan, no one can doubt that a primary threat to our security is now posed by groups acting outside formal states, or from places where no state functions at all. It is no longer possible to ignore distant and misgoverned parts of a world without borders, where chaos is a potential neighbour anywhere from Africa to Afghanistan. For terrorists are strongest where states are weakest. Osama bin Laden and the al-Qaida network find safe havens in those places where the collapse of responsible government and civil society have been brought about by conflict, poverty, ethnic and racial tensions, exploitation, corruption, poor governance, malign external interference or just plain neglect.

The global order conceived in the wake of the Second World War was not designed to deal with these failed states. The United Nations is made up of states, for example, and international law traditionally regulated relations between states. This system worked well enough to ensure that over the last 50 years many of us in Europe enjoyed the longest period of sustained peace in our history. Where the chief cause of war in the first half of the 20th century was aggression by states, in the second we built up a framework for managing sovereignty, through NATO and the EU, which made it relatively rare.

Yet increasingly nowadays, conflict arises where no functioning state exists. Only ten out of roughly 120 wars in the 1990s were between states, for example. Cambodia in the 1970s, Mozambique and Angola in the 1980s, Yugoslavia, Rwanda, Sierra Leone and the Democratic Republic of Congo in the 1990s, are all linked by one common denominator to Afghanistan today: that when we allow governments to fail, warlords, criminals, drugs barons or terrorists fill the vacuum.

The challenge posed by failed states, then, is not new, and for years the international community has devised strategies for dealing with them. The people of Sierra Leone are rebuilding their shattered economy and society. No one has been killed in conflict in Bosnia since 1995. East Timor will shortly become independent. Cambodia has a civil society where previously it had the Khmer Rouge. And against the odds, Mozambique is taking its place as a respected and progressive nation.

We have created mandates for peacekeeping, strategies for development assistance and responses to avert humanitarian catastrophes, not only from a sense of moral responsibility but out of a profound national interest. For an active and engaged global foreign policy is not some salve to liberal consciences, but a survival mechanism for all our societies.

It is in this context that we have to view the military, humanitarian and diplomatic activities of the international coalition against terrorism. The military action in Afghanistan which followed 11 September was not in itself the long-term answer to the threat of terrorism, but it was the essential first step. There could be no doubt about the clear and present danger to our way of life posed by Osama bin Laden and al-Qaida.

We could have chosen to do nothing, and by our inaction invite further attack. Instead we took the tough decision to embark on a military campaign. I respect the view of those who disagreed with this choice. But it is now clear that our choice was the right one, and that the campaign on all its fronts, military, diplomatic and humanitarian, has been vindicated by events.

Long before the terrorists hijacked the airliners that flew into the World Trade Centre and the Pentagon, they hijacked Afghanistan. Its people have been the biggest victims of the nexus formed by al-Qaida and the Taliban regime, through the denial of human rights, the complete absence of any strategy for economic development, and the obstruction of humanitarian aid.

The military defeat of the Taliban regime was therefore the liberation of the Afghan people. But there is now the imperative on the international community of a second liberation: liberating the Afghan people from the other scourges which have beset them for decades: fear, hunger, poverty and war.

I believe we can all agree on four principles to guide us as we help the Afghan people to rebuild their nation.

First, the future must be placed in the hands of the Afghan people. That is precisely what the Bonn Agreement last December has done. Exceeding all expectations, the representatives of the non-Taliban Afghan factions, some of whom have fought each other at different times in the last 20 years, thrashed out an agreement which puts Afghanistan on the path to peace.

No-one would claim that the interim administration, which took office on 22 December, is representative of the Afghan people in the widest sense. But within six months there will be an emergency Loya Jirga, the traditional Afghan assembly, opened by the former King of Afghanistan. This will include people drawn from a wide mix of groups: men – and women – in Afghanistan; refugees; civil society; Islamic scholars; traders; and prominent individuals. A broad-based transitional administration will emerge from the process; and eighteen months later, a full Loya Jirga is to agree a new constitution, under which free and fair elections will be held for a fully representative government.

If we have learned anything from the last 150 years of Afghan history, it is surely that solutions imposed from outside will not work. Of course the international community should provide assistance to help create the conditions for an indigenous government. Any administration must also respect internationally agreed norms of behaviour, towards other states and towards its own citizens. No regime will be sustainable unless it commands broad consent among those whom it governs. Yet within this essential framework, the form of government and the process that leads to its establishment should both be up to the Afghan people themselves.

My second principle is that we need an international coalition for Afghanistan's future. A pre-condition for the stability of any new government is not only the assent of its own people but also the support of its neighbours and the global community. Competition among the powers has always been Afghanistan's curse. Britain has no right to point the finger of blame, after we intrigued and fought with Russia for influence during the 19th century 'Great Game'. The intervention of different powers during the Cold War did no good either. Sometimes Afghan leaders themselves intrigued with outsiders. The victims were always the Afghan people.

What they need is an international consensus about the way forward. Now for the first time in three decades, there is agreement among the five permanent members of the UN Security Council, and among Afghanistan's neighbours, on the need for a broad-based, self-sustaining government. We shall all be working to reduce tensions and mutual suspicions in the region. Afghanistan should come to know the outside world as a benign, not threatening, influence.

My third principle is that the United Nations should play the leading role in any transition. Through humanitarian aid and other programmes, it already has unrivalled experience of Afghanistan. It also has behind it the relevant experience of helping to rebuild shattered communities in Cambodia, East Timor and Kosovo. Only the UN has the global reach, the instruments and the expertise to provide effective relief and reconstruction in Afghanistan, although it will need to do this in active partnership with committed states.

This crisis has proved, more than ever, that we need the UN. All countries should be ready to devote the resources it requires to carry out its broad range of tasks across the world. Already, the UN Secretary-General, Kofi Annan, and his Special Representative, Lakhdar Brahimi, have played a crucial role in bringing the Bonn negotiations to their remarkable conclusion.

My fourth principle is that we must be prepared to devote the resources and the political will needed to complete the task. This is a country which has known little but war, bloodshed and chaos for a generation. A quarter of all children do not make it to their fifth birthday. A third are orphans. Half are malnourished. There are many immediate tasks.

But we should also be prepared for the long haul. The international community has a role to play in protecting the fledgling institutions of the interim administration and providing a secure environment. The UK's leading role in the early months of the International Stability Assistance Force in and around Kabul is essential to the long-term success of reconstruction.

The redevelopment of Afghanistan will be a huge undertaking. It cost $5 billion to rebuild Bosnia but Afghanistan has four times the population, and reconstruction could take five to ten years to complete. We have to be ready to bear the cost. If we do not, the price will be far greater in terms of terrorist atrocities, lives lost and economies disrupted.

This crisis has also shown how our responsibility to the people of Afghanistan coincides with our duty to citizens at home. Bringing order out of chaos is one of the great tasks of foreign policy for the new century.

During the Cold War, some in the West drew inspiration from the domino theory: arguing that if Communism were not stopped in Korea, Vietnam, Nicaragua, or Angola, it would topple neighbouring countries and eventually reach us. Historians may argue about whether the domino theory really applied to Communism, but I have no doubt that it does apply to the chaos of failed states. In the 1990s the collapse of the Democratic Republic of Congo sucked in countries throughout the Great Lakes region of Africa. One of the biggest obstacles to peace in Sierra Leone was continuing violence in neighbouring Liberia. Even now any slide back into ethnic conflict in the former Yugoslavia could affect the whole region. An Afghanistan in chaos remains a threat to its neighbours in Pakistan, Iran and Central Asia, whose stability is already undermined by the drugs trade and the refugee crisis.

The fight against terrorism is different from the Cold War, which pitted two ideologies against one another in a battle for supremacy. This is a struggle in which all legitimate governments are on the same side. Our aim is to welcome Afghanistan back into the family of nation states, as a fully-fledged member of the international community. We want to see an independent, sovereign Afghanistan, functioning as a part of the global economy, generating wealth and welfare for its entire people. Rebuilding Afghanistan will be the next vital step towards a victory in which we all can share – victory over terrorism, victory over poverty and victory over chaos.

Jack Straw is Foreign Secretary of Great Britain.

12 A New Global Configuration

Fred Halliday

There are two predictable, and nearly always mistaken, responses to any great international upheaval: one is to say that everything has changed, the other is to say that nothing has changed. We have heard much of both in the aftermath of 11 September 2001, just as, a decade or so earlier, the same two polar positions were articulated after the earthquakes of that time, the collapse of the Berlin Wall, the Kuwait war and the dissolution of Yugoslavia.

11 September did not change everything: the map of the world with its 200 or so states, the global pattern of economic and military power, the relative distribution of democratic, semi-authoritarian and tyrannical states remains much the same. Many of the greatest threats to the world, and many of the problems which are least susceptible to traditional forms of state control (the environment, migration, the drugs trade, AIDS), long pre-dated 11 September. The 40 or so societies that are riven by war, from Colombia to Palestine, remain so. In a more specific sense, some of the changes that have become evident since 11 September were already incipient: the assertion of US power by the Bush administration, the rhetoric of cultural conflict coming out of both western and Islamic societies and intervention by OECD states to offset an anticipated recession.

Yet this recognition of continuity downplays the degree to which the attacks on the US 'homeland' have reshaped, or promise to reshape, the world in which we live. That some of these changes are evolutionary, reformist, rather than revolutionary, or absolute, does not diminish their importance. One can indeed suggest that it is reform, at least as much as revolution, which has in modern times done most to remodel the world. These are early days yet, and the conflict which 11 September spotlit, but did not begin, has many a year to run. But, in summary terms, there are at least five major ways in which the world after 11 September, and the world that we could have anticipated had 11 September not happened, are now different places.

First, there has been a marked increase in the focus and assertion of US power. The USA was, prior to 11 September, the dominant world power in every significant sense, with the possible exception of football. Yet it was uncertain as to how to exert this power, wavering between a multilateral approach, favoured by Clinton, and quite tenaciously pursued by his administration, and the unilateral, which is not the same as isolationist, policy favoured by Bush. The signs of that unilateralism were evident enough in the first few months: rejection of Kyoto, stalling on OECD regulation of tax havens, sliding out of chemical warfare conventions, NMD, sneering at the UN to name but some. 11 September has forced the Bush administration to reverse some of these policies and stall on others.

More importantly, however, it has led much of the rest of the world to seek to work more closely with the USA. Washington has, in this crisis, cashed in its power: when the call for co-operation comes, it has proven hard to refuse. Here lies the second of the great changes brought about by 11 September: some US allies have moved further away, notably Saudi Arabia, but the overall diplomatic balance sheet has been to the USA's advantage. Russia has, with its own benefit in mind, considered strategic and political collaboration with Washington. China too, to the alarm of some in the Middle East, who look to it as the only permanent member of the UN Security Council not to have a colonial past, joined the counter-terrorist campaign.

Against this, however, lies the third of the outcomes of 11 September, the consolidation, to a degree latent but not present before that date, of a global coalition of feeling against the USA. The basis of much orthodox theory of international relations is the concept 'balance of power': this means not an equal distribution of power, but a self-correcting mechanism whereby, if one state becomes too strong, others form a countervailing alliance against it. This happened in response to Napoleon in the 1800s and to Hitler in the 1940s. This version of balance of power did not work in the period since the end of the Cold War: there was no countervailing bloc of military, or economic, powers. Rather everyone seemed to want to join the US bloc and its associated international institutions, like NATO and the WTO.

However, if states band-wagon, popular opinion does not. At the level of popular feeling across the world, and not just in the Muslim world, a kind of countervailing balance of affect is taking shape. Hence the opposition of much of Latin America to support for the US campaign, widespread objections in East Asia and in (normally anti-Muslim) India. Loosely associated with globalisation, this antipathy to US hegemony too will not easily go away.

A fourth dimension is that of management of the global economy. 11 September has, by depressing certain important sectors of the market – airlines, tourism, oil, insurance – and by spreading a wider lack of confidence on the part of investors and consumers, accentuated the trend towards recession that was already evident. In the energy field, it has pushed down global demand for oil – there is now surplus capacity of around three million barrels of oil a day, with world output at around 75 million: this has precipitated not only a fall in oil prices, with no evident floor in sight, but also led to a potential price war between OPEC and the main non-OPEC producers (Russia, Norway, Mexico).

On the consumer side, there is renewed concern to reduce dependence on the oil of the Gulf, site of two thirds of the world's reserves, but now felt to be a region of enduring instability: non-Gulf producers, notably Russia, the Caspian states and Venezuela are pressing their case. Russia appears to have got some of what it wants, including an interest in any western plans to build a pipeline from the Caspian to Turkey outside Russian control. The Caspian states, notably Azerbaijan and Kazakhstan, are offering military and oil co-operation to the USA: but their own regimes may not be the most long-lasting. As for Venezuela, its ideal strategic location, in the western hemisphere, is for the moment offset by US anger at President Chavez's independent foreign policy, which has included criticism of the action in Afghanistan.

The most important economic shift, above all, is that 11 September has brought the state, and not least the US state, back into the management of the world economy: neo-liberal faith in the market, already frayed, has now been further eroded as the governments of the developed world promise to subsidise ailing sectors, use fiscal adjustment and lower interest rates to offset the crisis. One open question is how all this will affect the longer-term strength of the euro: the stability pact is already under pressure, and George Bush is not likely to worry much about what happens to this putative rival to the dollar. But the reversal of state policy across the OECD, through state and international financial institutional intervention, is remarkable.

In terms of regional power politics, the fifth dimension of change, the area most affected is that of West Asia. Pakistan seems to have been able to talk itself out of its isolation, and many hundreds of millions of debt, by switching to the US side. Provided the military regime of General Musharraf holds, it will be able to enjoy improved relations with the outside world: a stable Afghanistan would open up the prospect of the oil and gas pipelines of Central Asia coming southwards to Pakistani ports. Iran benefited in the short run: its relations with the UK and even the USA improved, and Foreign Minister Kharrazi met Colin Powell in New York. The warming of relations with the USA has, however, been short-lived.

The situation for the Arab world is rather different. Any further US campaign against al-Qaida will involve operations, overt or in the shadows, against its networks in two other countries, and ones where the state is weak or non-existent: Yemen and Somalia. For its part, the Iraqi regime knows that it too may be on the target list for US action: success in Kabul seems to have emboldened the US hawks on this matter. Europeans will try to restrain Washington, but action against

Iraq must remain a strong possibility. The Arab states of the Gulf are also in an uncomfortable situation, given the rise of pro-al-Qaida sentiment amongst young people in recent years. Saudi Arabia, above all, finds itself with a population that is strongly anti-American and which is increasingly critical of the ruling family because of unemployment and the elite's disproportionate take of oil and investment revenues. It has tried to offset this by reducing co-operation with the USA but has, in so doing, deeply antagonised the country on which it relies for its ultimate survival.

Time has, in a way, overtaken the cautious and often indecisive rulers of these oil-producing states. Washington may belatedly be getting the military facilities, and some of the tracer information on terrorist suspects and finances, it has asked for, but no president will find it easy to risk American lives to defend the House of Saud. Strategists in Washington are already thinking the unthinkable: if Saudi Arabia enters a serious crisis it may break up, as did two other states formed around the same time in the 1920s, Yugoslavia and the USSR. The question then becomes how to preserve the western, and global, economic interest in the oil and gas regions of the East without remaining embroiled in their domestic politics. It has not come to this yet, but it may.

Finally, the overall context for these changes, and for that which was in any case in train, is that of globalisation: while 11 September challenges some aspects of globalisation, notably a sense of rising global optimism in culture and economics, and freedom of movement for travellers and migrants, it has also given the opportunity for a more sober, and perhaps therefore sustainable, model of globalisation to be discussed. The institutions of global financial and macro-economic management will now be put to the test and given greater political support. Some greater urgency may, as was evident in the WTO meeting in Doha, enter discussion of global trade liberalisation and an improved distribution of wealth.

These policy issues are, however, taking place within a context defined by another set of controversies, and options, about values. The most obvious of these concerns the question of culture, and of universal or relative values. 11 September did not settle this question, but it has thrown the relativist, or communitarian, argument onto the defensive: on the one hand, as public argument in west and east has shown, the claim that there is one communal or traditional interpretation of text of belief is questionable; on the other, the invocation of cultural difference to legitimate criminal acts, or culturally phrased denial of responsibility and international obligation, is a bit harder to make.

There has also been an important shift, of great relevance in the aftermath of 11 September, about who is responsible for the upholding or violation of human rights. For a long time the answer was that this was the responsibility of states. But the 'non-state', be it the family, the tribe, the vicinity, or the self-proclaimed representative of the oppressed, is also responsible for, and often guilty of, human rights violations. Debates on, for example, violations of the rules of war or violence against women or racism have highlighted the combined responsibility of states and societies for human rights violations.

All of this has been made more difficult, prior to and subsequent to the US attacks, by the ever-widening scope of what are termed 'human rights' issues: a concern with the political rights of individuals has been matched by a commitment to social and economic rights, and, by extension, to the rights of collective groups, be these nations, women, children, refugees or disabled people. In addition, the scope of human rights concern, and activism, has also come to include what were earlier seen as separate issues, encoded in the Geneva Conventions of 1949, binding states, and the 1977 Additional Protocols, involving opposition groups, about the legitimate uses of violence.

This set of interrelated ethical and rights issues has, however, demonstrated that while no policy can neglect these questions, the certitude that there is one simple answer on human rights grounds, or one clear 'ethical' option, may be misleading. Those involved in distributing humanitarian assistance may have to buy off warlords, and indicted war criminals, with percentages of fuel, food and medicine. Those concerned with the rights of individuals, not least women, may have to override the supposedly 'authentic' or 'traditional' values of religions and communities. Indeed a more robust, and critical, stand towards the claims of community and 'difference' may be one desirable consequence of the more edgy human rights debate prompted by 11 September.

Much has been made of the challenge posed by 11 September to globalisation. It can be argued that it has weakened the liberal optimism that underlay globalisation, not least with regard to security of travel. But it may also be a challenge that brings out a stronger, more resilient commitment to globalisation. It has reminded those who, in a rush of liberal or cosmopolitan optimism, or in a semi-anarchist radical critique of global institutions, may have forgotten that without global security, and a security sustained by capable and determined powers, there will be no globalisation at all. A commitment to military security, combined with a broader but unflinching commitment to democratic and secular values, is a pre-requisite for any long-run resistance to terrorist attack. That sober but pertinent message may be one of the positive outcomes of the upheavals of the autumn of 2001.

Fred Halliday is Professor of International Relations at LSE. He is the author of *The World at 2000* (Palgrave) and *Two Hours That Shook the World: September 11 2001, Causes and Consequences* (Saqi).

PART V

The Contours of a World Community

13 Terror and Solidarity[1]

Ulrich Beck

The Global terrorism has opened a new chapter in the history of *World Risk Society* (Beck 1986, 1999) by giving a new impetus to its political dynamic. We have to distinguish clearly between the attack itself and the terrorist threat that was universalised through it. What is politically decisive is not so much risks as the *perception* of risks. What men *fear* to be real is real in its consequences.

Capitalism is premised on optimism about the future, which is why a sudden collective belief in a terrorist threat can shove a wobbling world economy over the edge into recession. When people see the world as one big terrorist threat, it renders them incapable of action. The most potent impact of terrorist attacks is that fear spreads far beyond the act of violence: this is the first trap the terrorists have set. The second is that the perceived risk of terrorism is being exploited by politicians to set up new security measures that threaten individual and democratic liberties – in other words, the very things which give modern society its superiority. If we face a choice between freedom or survival then it's already too late because, to be realistic, the majority of people in that case would decide against freedom.

The most powerful force the West has to fear is fear itself. So the greatest danger comes not from the terrorist risk but from its perception, which sets off a cycle of fantasies of danger and countermeasures to ward it off, both of which rob modern society of its ability to act. The simplest antidote to this may be a cynical look at the recent past. Think for a moment about how many "ends of the world" we've already experienced and lived through: Seveso, Chernobyl, global warming, mad cow disease. And now anthrax.

The question that terrorism raises, of how much freedom and how much security, is really another form of the world risk society's central question: how much certainty – its acknowledgement and valuation – is necessary in order to survive? Security comes at a cost. But what is unclear so far is if the costs really produce more security. So we need accountable information on how much security we are gaining – if any! – at the expense of what curtailment of liberty.

The question has been repeatedly asked, "What could unite the world?" And the hypothetical answer sometimes given is, "an attack from Mars". In a sense, that was just what this was, an attack from our inner Mars. And it worked as predicted. Although in historical terms this has only been the blink of eye so far, the warring camps and nations of the world have united against the common foe of global terrorism. Such unity can, of course, easily end with increasing military action, especially if it is judged to be unsuccessful.

It is precisely the universalism of this terrorist threat that has forged alliances between opposing camps, damped regional conflicts, and made it both possible and necessary to redraw the political map of the world. It is breathtaking how quickly and completely the priorities of US foreign policy have changed. Until recently, the thoughts and actions of Washington were focused on its intention to erect a national missile defence system. But we've heard very little of that lately. Instead, the insight seems to have been appreciated that even the most perfect missile defence couldn't have stopped this attack, and that US security lies not in going it alone down the high road of technology, but rather in the high politics of a global alliance. The rivalries with Moscow and Beijing have been played down, at least for the moment, in face of the fact that the 'defence' of the United States' domestic security in Afghanistan demands cooperation with Russia.

The power of universality, the fact that everyone feels at risk, has also suddenly opened up new possibilities of action in Europe. Rivalries have receded and commonality has come to the fore, not only within Europe, but between Europe and the US. It's a bad time to be a eurosceptic.

So what makes political action possible in the age of globalisation? My answer is: the perceived globality of risk. In an age where trust and faith in God, class, nation and government are forfeit, humanity, expressed through fear, is the last strong resource for making new bonds. Repeatedly in recent years we have seen how this has melted through the iron verities of national and international politics and allowed us to reshape them. And each time we are shocked at how quickly it happens, as if it has never happened before. We have to distinguish carefully between the immediate danger, the risk of the danger, and the systemic dangers that arise from the risk. Each level multiplies the last. It multiplies the people affected, and it multiplies the effect on society and politics. And in the end the decisive risks – and opportunities – for global risk society are most often the political side-effects of the actual danger to life and limb. What has happened right now is that the perceived risk of global terrorism has produced a quasi-revolutionary situation in world politics. And as such, it can be guided to very different ends. It could mean the end of the unilateralism and isolationism of US foreign policy, and a unifying foreign policy mission that tames national and regional conflicts and rivalries; or it could mean a 'crusade' that produces new squads of terrorists in its wake. It could also mean the loss of important freedoms, and protectionism, nationalism, and the demonisation of the culturally Other.

World risk society is a 'revolutionary' society. The terrorist attack on globalisation has had exactly the opposite effect that it intended. It has pushed us into a new phase of globalisation, the globalisation of politics, the moulding of states into transnational co-operative networks. Once more the rule has been confirmed that resistance to globalisation only accelerates it. Anti-globalisation activists don't only share their advanced means of communication with globalisation's proponents. They also operate on the basis of global rights, global markets, global mobility and global networks. They both think and act in global terms, and use them to awaken global awareness and a global public. And one can't help but notice that the anti-globalisation terrorists of 11 September seem to have chosen a target precisely because it would look striking on the cover of a newsmagazine. They also seem to have assumed that it would be natural that the destruction of the two towers would be experienced everywhere on earth at the same time though the televisual present we co-inhabit.

No doubt, in the aftermath of the terrorist attack, the state is back, and for the oldest Hobbesian reason – the provision of security. Around the world we will see governments becoming more powerful, more intrusive and more active – not only in anti-terrorist alliances but also in relation to the challenges of globalisation, its impacts and risks. This will not please civil libertarians and human rights activists, but it will not matter. Because at the same time the two dominant ideas about the state – the idea of the *national* state, and the idea of the *neoliberal* state – have both lost their reality, their necessity. Neoliberalism and the idea of the free market were supposed to hold the keys to the future. Over the last two decades they have grown into a hegemonic force. And maybe it is too soon to speak of the end of neoliberalism. But global terrorism has given us a taste of the kind of risks we can expect in a globalised future. And suddenly, in this time of dramatic global conflict, neoliberalism's fundamental postulate, that state and politics should be replaced by the market, seems absurdly unconvincing. To the question of whether the 40 billion dollars that the US government requested from Congress for the war against terrorism didn't contradict the neoliberal creed to which the Bush Administration subscribes, its spokesman replied laconically: 'National security comes first.'

But national security is no longer national security in the simple conventional sense. This is the second big lesson of the terrorist attack. Of course, there have always been alliances. But the decisive difference about this global alliance is that its purpose is to preserve *internal*, rather than external, security. And with that, all the taken-for-granted distinctions that make up our standard picture of the modern state – the borders that divide domestic from international, the police from the military, crime from war and war from peace – are overthrown. They all have to be renegotiated in our new situation and with new purposes in mind. But those old distinctions defined the nation state. Without them, it is a zombie idea. It still looks like it's alive, but it's dead.

It used to be that foreign policy was a matter of choice, not necessity. Today, instead of an either/or, we face a this-as-well-as-that: foreign and domestic policy, national security and international co-operation are all now interlocked. The only way to deal with global terror is also the only way to deal with global warming, immigration, poison in the food chain and organised crime. In all these cases, national security is transnational cooperation. It's a counterintuitive proposition, but in order to pursue their national interests, states have to denationalise and transnationalise themselves. They have to broker away parts of their sovereignty in order to control their national destiny in a globalised world. After the terror attack "terrorist sleepers" were identified in Hamburg and many other places. Therefore German domestic policy is now an important part of US domestic and foreign policy, as well as the now interwoven domestic, foreign, security and defence policies of France, Pakistan, Great Britain, and Russia.

Is Germany at war? Max Weber maintained that the power to declare war or peace was one of the essential features of a state. If it doesn't have a monopoly over war and peace, it isn't a state. I am a resident of Munich. Who represented the people of Munich in the decision on war and peace? The city council? The Bavarian state government? The German parliament? The federal chancellor? The European parliament? The European Commission? The NATO high command? President Bush? The UN Security Council? The rules may seem clear, but the reality increasingly is not. The power to decide between war and peace is no longer a matter for an individual state acting autonomously. Sovereignty and the state, which for Max Weber composed an indivisible unity, have been growing apart for some time. But we still need to grasp conceptually and politically what it means to say that a state's capacity for action can vary independently of its sovereignty.

The global terrorist threat has opened a new era of transnational and multilateral co-operation. It is leading not to a renaissance of nation states, but to the accelerated development of what I call *transnational co-operation states*. The national point of view is an obstacle to the reinvention of politics in the age of globalisation. This has been dramatically spelled out with regard to domestic security. Every day is revealing some new way in which the borders that once defined the nation state are simultaneously vanishing and being transnationally renegotiated, refixed. This discovery can just as well be applied to the problem of global poverty or human rights or the injured human dignity of the postcolonial world.

There are at least two different ideal types of transnational cooperation state: the *surveillance state* and the *cosmopolitan state*. Surveillance states threaten to use the new power of co-operation to build themselves into fortress states, in which security and military concerns will loom large and freedom and democracy will shrink. Already we hear about how western societies have got so used to peace and wellbeing that they lack the necessary vigour to distinguish friends from enemies. And that priorities will have to change. And that some of our precious rights will have to be sacrificed for the sake of security. This attempt to construct a western citadel against the numinous Other has already sprung up in every country and will only increase in the years to come. It is the sort of thing out of which a democratic authoritarianism might someday arise, a system in which maintaining flexibility towards the world market would be premised on increasing domestic rigidity. Globalisation's winners would get neoliberalism, and globalisation's losers would get the back of the hand: a heightened fear of foreigners, born of fear of terrorism, and spiked with the poison of racism.

But what are we fighting *for* when we fight against global terrorism? My answer is this: for a culture of humanity in which different traditions can coexist without ignoring their differences; in other words, for the right to be at once cosmopolitan and local, which is fundamentally based on the recognition of the otherness of the others. And what we need is a system of states that makes it possible to take that responsibility.

National states present a threat to the inner complexity, the multiple loyalties and the social fluidity that the age of globalisation has caused to lap across their borders. And conversely, they can't but see such fuzzing of borders as a threat to their existence. Cosmopolitan states, by contrast, emphasise the necessity of solidarity with foreigners both inside and outside the national borders. They do this by connecting self-determination with responsibility for (national and non-national) Others. It is not a matter of limiting or negating self-determination. On the contrary, it is a matter of freeing self-determination from its national cyclops vision and connecting it to the world's concerns. Cosmopolitan states struggle not only against terror, but against the *causes* of terror. They seek to regain and renew the power of politics to shape and persuade, and they do this by seeking the solution to global problems that are even now burning humanity's fingertips, but which can't be solved by individual nations on their own.

Cosmopolitan states can theoretically be founded on the principle of the national indifference of the state. Similar to the way that, in the 16th century, the Peace of Westphalia ended the religious civil war we call the Thirty Years War through the separation of church and state, so the separation of state and nation can be the solution to the world and civil wars of the 20th century. Just as the secular state finally made possible the peaceful coexistence of multiple religions side by side, the cosmopolitan state could provide the conditions for multiple national and religious identities to exist side by side through the principle of constitutional tolerance.

We should seize this opportunity to reconceive the European political project as an experiment in the building of cosmopolitan states. And a cosmopolitan Europe, whose political force would emerge directly out of the worldwide struggle against terrorism, also out of the affirmation and taming of European national complexity; something that preserved all its niches and characters but removed from them their threat: now that would be a *Weltbürger*-society worth fighting for.

Ulrich Beck is Professor of Sociology at the University of Munich.

[1] A version of this essay appeared in the *New Statesman* on November 5th, 2001.

14 The Power of World Community

Tony Blair

The acts of evil perpetrated on 11 September shocked the whole world. But beyond the human horror and landscapes of wreckage in New York and Washington, September 11 jolted us because it brought home the true meaning of globalisation in a way that no change in economics or technology ever could.

The reality of globalisation was gradually becoming apparent throughout the 1990s. It has already transformed our economies and our way of life forever. The impact has been as far-reaching as either the agricultural or industrial revolutions were in the eighteenth and nineteenth centuries. Participation in global markets has become central to every nation's prosperity. But it is not simply an economic phenomenon. It finds expression too in political change and in international challenges to the security of both individual nations and groups of them.

And in this respect, it was the events of 11 September which finally shattered the illusion that we can exist in a bubble, isolated from the rest of the world and its problems – the illusion that we can enjoy the good life of the West irrespective of the state of the rest of the world.

In this globalised world, once chaos and strife have got a grip on a region or a country, trouble is soon exported. Such regions and countries can become centres for trafficking in weapons, drugs and people; havens for criminal organisations; and sanctuaries for terrorists. It was, after all, a dismal camp in the foothills of Afghanistan that gave birth to the murderous assault on the sparkling heart of New York's financial centre.

But action against terrorists – effective though it has been in

Afghanistan – only takes us so far. Such military and security action needs to be backed with political change that tackles the conditions under which terrorism and international organised crime flourish or are tolerated. The dragon's teeth are planted in the fertile soil of wrongs unrighted, of disputes left to fester for years or even decades, of failed states, of poverty and deprivation.

In today's interdependent world, there can be no secure future for any of us unless we manage globalisation with greater justice. 11 September showed us that isolationism is no longer a credible posture for any nation. Co-operation across borders is a necessity of modern political and economic life. We are all internationalists now.

And so, against the background of military action and fast-moving events, a broader shift is emerging. The power of community is re-asserting itself. And this must be the greater memorial to the dead of September 11 – not simply the punishment of those responsible, but a new international mood of hope and understanding, and above all, justice and prosperity for the poor and dispossessed.

I believe we will succeed only if we start to develop a doctrine of international community based on the principle of enlightened self-interest – on the recognition that self-interest and our mutual interests are today inextricably woven together.

It is a recognition which will transform domestic as well as international politics, because globalisation shrinks the distance between domestic and international issues. Indeed it often renders them identical: tackling terrorism in the USA means dealing with issues on the ground in the mountains of Afghanistan; bringing economic security to just one town in northern England means addressing the international machinery of global finance. The international has become domestic and the domestic international.

The issue is not how to stop globalisation. That is in any case futile: as the Chinese proverb has it, "no hand can block out the sun." The issue is rather how we use the power of community to bring the benefits of globalisation to all.

We need to be clear about what we mean by justice and community. It is not a question of trampling on local sensibilities: the values of liberty, the rule of law, human rights and a pluralist society are universal and worthy of respect in every culture.

To spread them and to make the whole world more stable, we need a new international framework to agree and enforce international rules. In the wake of World War II, we developed an impressive series of international institutions to cope with the strains of rebuilding a devastated world: Bretton Woods, the United Nations, NATO, and the EU. To survive and remain useful today, they will have to adapt.

The Asian financial crisis and recent problems in Argentina have shown, for a start, that our international financial system is not working as it should. Bretton Woods was set up for the post-war world; we now need a new financial architecture. Greater transparency should be the keystone of reform: transparency about individual countries' economic policies, through adherence to new codes of conduct on monetary and fiscal policy; about individual companies' financial positions through new internationally agreed accounting standards and a new code of corporate governance; and greater openness too about IMF and World Bank policies.

We also need improved financial supervision both in individual countries, through stronger and more effective peer group reviews, and internationally through the foundation of a new Financial Stability Forum. And we need more effective ways of resolving economic crises. The new contingent credit line at the IMF will assist countries pursuing sensible economic reforms and prevent damaging contagion. But we should also think creatively about how the private sector can help to resolve short-term financial crises.

Success in the new WTO round is vital to the strength of this global economic order. Success will mean increased trade flows and rising living standards around the world. Failure would mean a retreat into protectionism and isolationism, the swiftest road to poverty. But that international system must be based on rules. That means accepting the judgements of international organisations even when you do not like them.

The UN is also in much need of reform. We are lucky to have the leadership of a highly talented and reforming Secretary-General. We need to back him in his reforms and give him the practical support he needs – for example, by bringing to a close the long drawn-out negotiations on UN Security Council reform, so that it becomes truly representative and effective in its operation. We need to find a new way to make the UN and its Security Council work if we are not to return to the deadlock that undermined the effectiveness of the Security Council during the Cold War.

This kind of reform raises the question of when and how far the international community should get actively involved in conflicts. Non-interference has long been considered an important principle of international order, and it is not one we should jettison. But it must be qualified in important respects. Acts of genocide can never be a purely internal matter. When oppression produces massive flows of refugees which unsettle neighbouring countries, then they can properly be described as "threats to international peace and security".

Now, after years of turmoil, Afghanistan has a real chance of stability and peace. The international community cannot stop at military action; it must also help Afghanistan transform itself into a modern pluralist state. Alone, the interim government faces a huge challenge, but with the partnership and solidarity of the international community, Afghanistan can look forward to a more stable future.

The confrontation between Israelis and Palestinians, that has brought so much suffering to both sides, must be tackled with renewed urgency. The Middle East Peace Process must be re-started. First steps in mutual confidence and security on both sides must be made on the basis of two fixed principles: a viable Palestinian state, and a state of Israel accepted fully by its Arab neighbours. If Israel is to recognise that the Palestinians will have their own state, it is only right that the Arab world explicitly and clearly recognises Israel's right to exist secure within its own borders. We want to work with all countries that want to end the violence and promote a solution that is just for both Palestinians and Israelis.

In Africa, there is the best hope for change in a generation. A group of African countries have put forward the New Partnership for Africa's Development (NEPAD) to tackle conflict and governance issues and to boost economic growth and investment in people. For the UK, our partnership with Africa must be a pillar of our foreign policy, built on mutual self-interest. Our partnership should cover the full range of issues that inhibit Africa's potential. We need aid to invest in creating capable states that encourage economic growth and invest in public services. But we also need wider policies to address low investment, to improve peacekeeping capacity, to tackle corruption and strengthen democracy.

In respect of Russia, common commitment to tackle terrorism after September 11 demonstrated a new partnership between Russia and the West. Central to that new relationship should be a step change in Russia-NATO relations. We also need a fresh economic approach, with the aim of creating in Europe a single economic space in which lasting prosperity and peace can flourish.

We will all benefit from a thriving Russia. We want a successful, prosperous Russia with which we can work in partnership.

I realise why people protest against globalisation. It is easy to feel powerless, overwhelmed, as if we were pushed to and fro by forces far beyond our control. But whether we like it or not, globalisation is a fact.

Since 11 September, countries have been rapidly revising their relations with others. The stakes are high: we need to get it right. Should we fail to do so, and subside into protectionism, narrow regionalism or even isolationism, we shall pay a heavy price.

But by the same token, the dynamism of globalisation and the speed of events makes this a moment of historic potential for creating international stability and peace, and for bringing economic development to parts of the world left behind. It is an opportunity to harness the power of community for the good of all, to create a world where people everywhere can see the chance of a better future through hard work and the creative power of the free citizen, not the violence and savagery of the fanatic. And that is an opportunity we should grasp with both hands.

Tony Blair is Prime Minister of the United Kingdom.

Also available from The Foreign Policy Centre

Individual publications should be ordered from
Central Books, 99 Wallis Road, London, E9 5LN
tel: 020 8986 5488, fax: 020 8533 5821
email: mo@centralbooks.com

To order online go to www.fpc.org.uk/reports

(Subscriptions are available from the Centre itself)

THE FOREIGN POLICY CENTRE MISSION STATEMENT

March 3rd 1999; Free, with £1 p+p, or free with any pamphlet.

'Likely to be controversial with Mandarins and influential with Ministers', **Financial Times**

THIRD GENERATION CORPORATE CITIZENSHIP

Simon Zadek
November 2001, £19.95; plus £1 p+p.
Kindly supported by Diageo and Friends Ivory & Sime

'Zadek strikes at the very heart of this debate', **Craig Cohon, Globelegacy**

THE PRO-EUROPEAN READER

Dick Leonard & Mark Leonard (editors)
Published by Palgrave November 2001, £16.99; plus £1 p+p.

'Here's a book full of cures for prejudice and phobia. Some of the antidotes are bold, some wry, some profound, some sharp – all short. The treatment is worth every Euro', **Neil Kinnock**

THE KIDNAPPING BUSINESS

Rachel Briggs
Kindly supported by Hiscox, Control Risks Group, ASM Ltd., Marsh Ltd. and SCR
March 2001, £14.95; plus £1 p+p

'A fascinating pamphlet', **Simon Jenkins, The Times**

THE FUTURE SHAPE OF EUROPE

Mark Leonard (editor)
Kindly supported by Adamson BSMG Worldwide; November 2000 £9.95; plus £1 p+p.

"The Europe of Nice is a building site waiting for new master builders. A booklet by The Foreign Policy Centre makes the point more eloquently than any polemicist", **Peter Preston, The Guardian**

NGO RIGHTS AND RESPONSIBILITIES:
A new deal for global governance

Michael Edwards, Director of Governance, Ford Foundation (writing personally)
In association with NCVO July 2000 £9.95; plus £1 p+p.

'Compelling and succinct', **Peter Hain, Minister of State, FCO**

GOING PUBLIC:
Diplomacy for the Information Society (interim report)

Mark Leonard and Vidhya Alakeson
May 16 2000 £9.95; plus £1 p+p.
Supported by the BBC World Service, The British Council, and the Design Council.

'An important new pamphlet...argues that the old ideas of British diplomacy must change profoundly', **Gavin Esler, The Scotsman**

AFTER MULTICULTURALISM

Yasmin Alibhai-Brown, The Foreign Policy Centre
May 2000 £9.95; plus £1 p+p.

'Yasmin is brave, intelligent and always worth reading', **Diane Abbott, MP, New Statesman**

RE-ENGAGING RUSSIA

John Lloyd
In association with BP Amoco 20th March 2000 £9.95; plus £1 p+p.

'Re-engaging Russia is excellent on where Russia's relationships with the West went wrong...thought-provoking, highly enjoyable, creative and timely', **Rt Hon Keith Vaz MP, Minister for Europe**

REINVENTING THE COMMONWEALTH

Kate Ford and Sunder Katwala
In association with the Royal Commonwealth Society
November 1999 £9.95; plus £1 p+p.

'Intelligent and wide-reaching', **The Times**

*'My first thought was "Why has it taken 50 years to start this debate?
Why aren't more developing countries leading it?'*, **Sharon Chetty,
The Sowetan**

TRADING IDENTITIES:
Why Countries and Companies Are Becoming More Alike

Wally Olins
October 1999 £9.95; plus £1 p+p.

'A fascinating pamphlet', **Peter Preston, The Guardian**

GLOBALIZATION – KEY CONCEPTS

David Held & Anthony McGrew, David Goldblatt & Jonathan Perraton
April 12th 1999 £4.95; plus £1 p+p

'An indispensable counterweight to optimists and pessimists alike',
Will Hutton

*'This is the agenda on which a new politics must be constructed and
new alliances forged'*, **Clare Short, Secretary of State for International
Development, New Statesman**

NETWORK EUROPE

Mark Leonard
In association with Clifford Chance; 10th September 1999 £9.95; plus £1 p+p

*'A radical agenda for reform from the government's favourite foreign
policy think-tank'*, **Stephen Castle, Independent on Sunday**

*'A welcome contribution to the important debate about Europe's
future'*, **Rt Hon Tony Blair MP, Prime Minister**

THE POSTMODERN STATE AND THE NEW WORLD ORDER
Robert Cooper
In association with Demos, 2nd edition

'Mr Cooper's pamphlet explains, lucidly and elegantly, how the emergence of what he calls the postmodern state has changed international relations', **New Statesman**

Subscribe to The Foreign Policy Centre

The Foreign Policy Centre offers a number of ways for people to get involved. Our subscription scheme keeps you up-to-date with our work, with at least six free publications each year and our quarterly newsletter, Global Thinking. Subscribers also receive major discounts on events and further publications.

Type of Subscription	Price
☐ Individuals	£50
☐ Organisations	£150
☐ Corporate and Libraries (will receive ALL publications)	£200

Please make cheques payable to **The Foreign Policy Centre**, indicating clearly your postal and email address and the appropriate package, and send to Subscriptions, The Foreign Policy Centre, Mezzanine Floor, Elizabeth House, 39 York Road, London SE1 7NQ. For further details, contact Rachel Briggs: rachel@fpc.org.uk

The Foreign Policy Centre Diplomatic Forum

The Foreign Policy Centre Diplomatic Forum is aimed at the key embassy players. It is an ideal way for embassies to keep up-to-date with the work of The Foreign Policy Centre and will provide a useful environment for ideas sharing.

Members will receive the following benefits:

- Special invitations to attend The Foreign Policy Centre annual Diplomatic Forum, which will be led by a high-profile speaker, bringing together key embassy players to address one or more of the foreign policy issues of the day
- Three free copies of every Foreign Policy Centre publication
- Three free copies of *Global Thinking*, The Foreign Policy Centre's newsletter
- VIP invitations for up to three embassy representatives to all Foreign Policy Centre public events
- Event reports from major Foreign Policy Centre events and seminars

Membership of The Foreign Policy Centre Diplomatic Forum is £500 per year. For further details, please contact Rachel Briggs, rachel@fpc.org.uk

The Foreign Policy Centre Business Partnership

The Foreign Policy Centre also runs a Business Partnership scheme, which aims to bring the business community to the heart of foreign policy thinking.

For more details about this scheme, please contact Rachel Briggs, rachel@fpc.org.uk